QUICK & EASY
MICROWAVING™
GROUND BEEF

Developed By The Kitchens Of The  MICROWAVE COOKING INSTITUTE®

Prentice Hall Press • New York

D1127626

PRENTICE HALL PRESS is a trademark of Simon & Schuster, Inc.

Library of Congress Cataloging-in-Publication Data

Quick & easy microwaving ground beef.

   (Quick & easy microwaving library ; 4)
   Includes index.
   1. Cookery (Beef) 2. Microwave cookery.
I. Microwave Cooking Institute. II. Title:
Quick and easy microwaving ground beef. III. Series.
TX749.Q53 1987   641.6'62   86-43155
ISBN 0-13-749425-4
Manufactured in the United States of America
10 9 8 7 6 5 4 3 2 1
First Prentice Hall Press Edition

Contents

Ground Beef 4

Ground Beef Basics 6

Sandwiches & Snacks 8

Soups & Stews 24

Sauces & Toppings 38

Meatballs 46

Meatloaf 60

Casseroles & One-dish Meals 78

Ground Beef

Ground beef has become a traditional menu item at millions of American tables. It offers an unusual combination of economy, nutritional value, and most of all versatility. Because ground beef is suited for appetizers, sandwiches, casseroles — even soups and stews — it is a rare household that does not consume ground beef at least once a week; in some homes it is a daily meal staple. And because it can be frozen and stored, a supply of ground beef in the freezer can greatly simplify your shopping chores.

Ground beef is categorized and sold according to its fat content. Extra-lean contains no more than 15% fat, while regular hamburger may contain up to 30%. The choice is yours: lean ground beef costs more, but shrinks less during cooking. Regular hamburger is economical, but tends to

lose volume as it cooks. Extra-lean is a good choice for dieters. Regular ground beef should be well-drained both during and after cooking.

In the past, some cooks have felt reluctant to use their microwave ovens to cook ground beef. In fact, microwaving can cut cooking times by 50% or more.

Ground beef also cooks more evenly in your microwave. This means that outside surfaces do not burn and brown the way they do in frying. If the traditional seared, browned surfaces are appealing to you, a microwave browning dish or brush-on browning agent may be used.

Quick & Easy Microwaving Ground Beef is a collection of more than 80 recipes, each developed and tested to match the way you cook today. Most recipes can be prepared in a few minutes; a few may take half-an-hour or more. The recipe selection in this book was founded on traditional ground beef favorites, and expanded to bring infinite variety to your menu planning.

What could possibly make more sense than combining the quickest and most versatile appliance in your kitchen with one of the most versatile foods available? *Quick & Easy Microwaving Ground Beef:* the possibilities are endless.

Storing Ground Beef

Fresh ground beef should be refrigerated for no longer than 24 hours before using, but it can be frozen and stored for 3 to 4 months without a noticeable loss of freshness.

Divide larger bulk packages of ground beef into smaller, more convenient 1 to 1½-lb. packages before freezing. To speed defrosting time, use shallow plastic freezer boxes, or shape ground beef into portions 1½ to 2 inches thick before wrapping in foil or freezer paper.

Form ground beef into patties to be used in burgers or Salisbury steaks, and layer between sheets of plastic wrap or wax paper. Wrap stacked patties in foil or freezer wrap before freezing. To use, remove as many patties as needed, then reseal the package.

Ground Beef Basics

How to Defrost Ground Beef

DEFROSTING GROUND BEEF	
Microwave at 50% (Medium):	Time:
1 lb.	3-5 minutes
2 patties (¼ lb. each)	3-5 minutes
4 patties (¼ lb. each)	4-6 minutes

1 Remove ground beef from the package and place in a 2-quart casserole. Divide the total defrosting time (as indicated in chart, left) into 3 equal segments.

How to Defrost Ground Beef Patties

Microwave frozen patties, 2 or 4 at a time (as directed in chart, above) or until burgers are still slightly icy in center. Let patties stand for 5 minutes to complete defrosting.

How to Brown Ground Beef Patties

Brush on a browning agent like soy sauce, teriyaki, bouquet sauce, barbecue sauce or gravy mix before microwaving if you prefer a browned appearance. Because they cook so quickly, microwaved hamburgers do not sear and brown the way they do conventionally.

2 Microwave ground beef in 3 segments. Remove defrosted portions of meat after each segment of defrosting time.

3 Break up the remaining ground beef before microwaving for last segment. If frozen portions still remain, let ground beef stand for 5 to 10 minutes to complete defrosting.

How to Microwave Grease-free Ground Beef

1 Speed cleanup by layering 4 paper towels in the bottom of a 2-quart casserole to absorb fat. Crumble 1 lb. of ground beef into casserole. Microwave at High for 4 to 7 minutes, or until meat is no longer pink, stirring gently to break apart 2 or 3 times during cooking.

2 Lift one side of the paper towels, allowing the ground beef to fall into the casserole. Discard paper towels. This method eliminates the need to drain ground beef during cooking.

Sandwiches & Snacks

These exciting variations will bring new life to old family favorites

Basic Hamburgers

1 lb. ground beef, crumbled
One or more of the following:
1 tablespoon prepared horseradish
1 tablespoon finely chopped onion
1 tablespoon catsup
1 tablespoon prepared barbecue sauce
1 teaspoon Worcestershire sauce
1 teaspoon prepared mustard
½ teaspoon seasoned salt
½ teaspoon chili powder
½ teaspoon celery salt
½ teaspoon Italian seasoning
¼ teaspoon garlic powder
¼ teaspoon onion powder
¼ teaspoon pepper

2 or 4 servings

Follow photo directions, right.

Total Cooking Time: 4½ to 7½ minutes

How to Microwave Basic Hamburgers

1 Combine the ground beef and the desired flavorings in a medium bowl. Divide the mixture into 4 equal portions and shape each portion into a 4-inch round patty. Arrange the patties on a roasting rack.

2 Microwave at High for 4½ to 7½ minutes, or until the meat is firm and no longer pink, turning the burgers over once during cooking time. (For 2 burgers, microwave at High for 2½ to 4½ minutes.)

Before Standing   After Standing

3 Let burgers stand, covered with wax paper, for 2 minutes before serving. (Burgers may appear slightly pink on top center after microwaving; pink areas will disappear during standing time.)

◄ Bacon Cheese Burgers

4 slices bacon
1 lb. ground beef
4 slices (¾ oz. each) pasteurized process
   American cheese

4 servings

1 Layer 3 paper towels on a plate. Arrange bacon slices on paper towels and cover with another paper towel. Microwave bacon at High for 3 to 6 minutes, or until crisp and golden brown. Break each piece in half and set aside.

2 Divide ground beef into 4 equal portions. Shape each portion into a 4-inch round patty. Arrange patties on a roasting rack and microwave at High for 4½ to 7½ minutes, or until meat is firm and no longer pink, turning burgers over once during cooking time. (For 2 burgers, microwave at High for 2½ to 4½ minutes.)

3 Arrange 2 bacon halves on top of each burger and top with a slice of cheese. Cover burgers with wax paper and let stand for 2 to 3 minutes, or until the cheese melts.

Total Cooking Time: 7½ to 13½ minutes

Vegie Burgers

Meat Mixture:
1 lb. ground beef, crumbled
½ cup alfalfa sprouts
¼ cup shredded carrot
2 teaspoons instant minced onion
1 teaspoon Worcestershire sauce
½ teaspoon dried basil leaves
¼ teaspoon salt
⅛ teaspoon pepper
4 slices (¾ oz. each) pasteurized process
   American cheese (optional)
Toppings:
   Thinly sliced tomato, onion or avocado

4 servings

1 Combine all the meat mixture ingredients in a medium bowl. Divide mixture into 4 equal portions and shape each portion into a 4-inch round patty. Arrange patties on a roasting rack and microwave at High for 4½ to 7½ minutes, or until the meat is firm and no longer pink, turning burgers over once during cooking time.

2 Top each burger with a slice of cheese. Cover burgers with wax paper and let stand for 2 to 3 minutes, or until cheese melts. Serve burgers in whole wheat buns with desired toppings.

Total Cooking Time: 4½ to 7½ minutes

Basic Salisbury Steak

1 lb. ground beef, crumbled
1 cup soft bread crumbs
1 large egg
3 tablespoons milk
1 teaspoon dried parsley flakes
½ teaspoon Worcestershire sauce
½ teaspoon salt
⅛ teaspoon garlic or onion powder
⅛ teaspoon pepper

4 servings

1 Combine all the ingredients in a medium bowl. Divide mixture into 4 equal portions. Shape each portion into a 4½ × 3-inch oval patty.

2 Arrange the patties on a roasting rack and microwave at High for 8 to 12 minutes, or until the meat is firm and no longer pink, turning patties over once during cooking time. Let steaks stand, covered with wax paper, for 2 minutes before serving.

Total Cooking Time: 8 to 12 minutes

Open-face Salisbury Steak ◄

Meat Mixture:
1 lb. ground beef
1 large egg
¼ cup finely chopped onion
¼ cup finely chopped green pepper
¼ cup unseasoned dry bread crumbs
1 medium carrot, shredded
1 tablespoon Worcestershire sauce
1 teaspoon seasoned salt
Gravy:
1 envelope (.87 oz.) brown gravy mix
1 cup cold water
2 English muffins, split and toasted

4 servings

1 Combine all the meat mixture ingredients in a medium bowl. Divide mixture into 4 equal portions. Shape each portion into a 4½ × 3-inch oval patty.

2 Arrange the patties on a roasting rack. Microwave at High for 8 to 12 minutes, or until the meat is firm and no longer pink, turning patties over once during cooking time. Let steaks stand, covered with wax paper.

3 Combine the brown gravy mix and the water in a 2-cup measure. Microwave at High for 1 to 3 minutes, or until the sauce thickens and bubbles, stirring after every minute of cooking time. Place each Salisbury steak on an English muffin half; top with gravy.

Total Cooking Time: 9 to 15 minutes

How to Microwave Basic Stuffed Burgers

1 Divide the ground beef into 8 equal portions. Shape each portion into a 4-inch round patty.

2 Divide cheese into 4 portions, and place 1 portion in the center of each of 4 patties. Top with remaining patties, and press edges together to seal. Arrange stuffed burgers on a roasting rack.

Basic Stuffed Burgers

1 lb. ground beef
½ cup finely shredded cheese

2 or 4 servings

Follow photo directions, below.

Total Cooking Time: 3 to 7 minutes

Quantity:	First Side:	Second Side:
2	2 minutes	1-3 minutes
4	3 minutes	3-4 minutes

Burger-shaping Tip:
To neatly and quickly shape ground beef into
burger patties and Salisbury steaks, place each
portion between sheets of plastic wrap and
press into desired shape.

3 Microwave at High, as directed in chart above, or until the meat is firm and no longer pink, turning burgers over once during cooking time.

4 Let burgers stand, covered with wax paper, for 2 minutes before serving. (Burgers may appear slightly pink on top center after microwaving; pink areas will disappear during standing time.)

15

Stuffed Italian Burgers

Meat Mixture:
- 1 lb. ground beef, crumbled
- 1 large egg
- 3 tablespoons seasoned dry bread crumbs
- 1 tablespoon prepared Italian dressing
- ½ teaspoon salt

Filling:
- ¼ cup seeded chopped tomato
- 2 tablespoons finely chopped onion
- 2 tablespoons finely chopped green pepper
- 1 tablespoon grated Parmesan cheese
- 1 tablespoon prepared Italian dressing
- 2 teaspoons seasoned dry bread crumbs
- ¼ teaspoon Italian seasoning

4 servings

1 Combine all the meat mixture ingredients in a medium bowl. Divide mixture into 8 equal portions and shape each portion into a 4-inch round patty. Set patties aside.

2 Combine all the filling ingredients in a small bowl. Divide mixture into 4 portions and place 1 portion in the center of each of 4 patties. Top with the remaining patties, and press edges together to seal.

3 Arrange stuffed burgers on a roasting rack. Microwave at High for 6 to 8 minutes, or until meat is firm and no longer pink, turning burgers over once during cooking time. Let burgers stand, covered with wax paper, for 2 minutes before serving.

Total Cooking Time: 6 to 8 minutes

Stuffed Pizza Burgers ▲

1½ lbs. ground beef
Filling:
- ¼ cup finely chopped pepperoni
- ¼ cup shredded mozzarella cheese
- 2 tablespoons chopped green pepper
- 1 tablespoon chopped onion

4 servings

1 Divide the ground beef into 8 equal portions. Shape each portion into a 4-inch round patty; set patties aside.

2 Combine all the filling ingredients in a small bowl. Divide mixture into 4 portions and place 1 portion in center of each of 4 patties. Top with the remaining patties, and press edges together to seal.

3 Arrange stuffed burgers on a roasting rack. Microwave at High for 6 to 8 minutes, or until meat is firm and no longer pink, turning burgers over once during cooking time. Let burgers stand, covered with wax paper, for 2 minutes before serving.

Total Cooking Time: 6 to 8 minutes

Stuffed Mushroom Burgers ▲

Meat Mixture:
- 1 lb. ground beef, crumbled
- 1 cup soft bread crumbs
- 1 large egg
- ½ teaspoon salt
- ⅛ teaspoon pepper

Filling:
- ⅓ cup canned sliced mushrooms
- ¼ cup sliced green onions
- 1 oz. cream cheese
- 1 teaspoon dried parsley flakes

4 servings

1 Combine all the meat mixture ingredients in a medium bowl. Divide mixture into 8 equal portions and shape each portion into a 4-inch round patty; set patties aside.

2 Place all the filling ingredients in a small bowl. Microwave at High for 15 to 30 seconds, or until the cream cheese is softened. Stir to combine ingredients.

3 Divide mixture into 4 portions and place 1 portion in the center of each of 4 patties. Top with the remaining patties, and press edges together to seal.

4 Arrange stuffed burgers on a roasting rack. Microwave at High for 6 to 8 minutes, or until meat is firm and no longer pink, turning burgers over once during cooking time. Let burgers stand, covered with wax paper, for 2 minutes before serving.

Total Cooking Time: 6¼ to 8½ minutes

Stuffed Burgers Mexican Style

1½ lbs. ground beef

Filling:
- 3 tablespoons shredded Cheddar cheese
- 3 tablespoons shredded Monterey Jack cheese
- 1 tablespoon canned or fresh chopped green chilies
- 1 tablespoon chopped black olives
- ⅛ teaspoon ground cumin
  Dash chili powder

4 servings

1 Divide the ground beef into 8 equal portions and shape each portion into a 4-inch round patty. Set patties aside.

2 Combine all the filling ingredients in a small bowl. Divide mixture into 4 portions and place 1 portion in the center of each of 4 patties. Top with the remaining patties, and press edges together to seal.

3 Arrange the stuffed burgers on a roasting rack. Microwave at High for 6 to 8 minutes, or until the meat is firm and no longer pink, turning burgers over once during cooking time. Let burgers stand, covered with wax paper, for 2 minutes before serving.

Total Cooking Time: 6 to 8 minutes

Open-face Pizza Burgers

1 lb. ground beef, crumbled
⅓ cup finely chopped onion
¼ cup chopped pepperoni
1 can (10¾ oz.) condensed tomato soup
2 tablespoons chopped pimiento-stuffed olives (optional)
¾ teaspoon dried oregano leaves
¼ teaspoon dried basil leaves
¼ teaspoon pepper
⅛ teaspoon garlic powder
4 English muffins, split and toasted
1 cup shredded mozzarella cheese, divided

8 servings

1 Place the ground beef, onion and pepperoni in a 2-quart casserole. Microwave at High for 4 to 7 minutes, or until the meat is no longer pink, stirring to break apart once during cooking time. Drain.

2 Stir in the remaining ingredients, except the muffins and cheese. Microwave at High for 6 to 10 minutes, or until the flavors are blended and mixture is slightly thickened.

3 Arrange 4 muffin halves on a paper-towel-lined plate. Top each muffin half with about ⅓ cup of the meat mixture and 1 tablespoon of the mozzarella cheese. If desired, sprinkle with grated Parmesan cheese.

4 Microwave pizza burgers at High for 1 to 2 minutes, or until the cheese melts, rotating plate once during cooking time. Repeat with remaining muffin halves.

Total Cooking Time: 12 to 21 minutes

Southern Barbecue Burgers

1½ lbs. ground beef, crumbled
1 cup chopped onion
¾ cup chopped celery or green pepper
1 can (10¾ oz.) condensed tomato soup
½ cup prepared barbecue sauce
2 teaspoons Worcestershire sauce
½ teaspoon salt
⅛ teaspoon cayenne

4 to 6 servings

1 Place the ground beef, onion and celery in a 2-quart casserole. Cover; microwave at High for 6 to 9 minutes, or until the meat is no longer pink and the vegetables are tender-crisp, stirring once or twice during cooking time. Drain.

2 Stir in the remaining ingredients. Microwave at High for 7 to 9 minutes, or until the flavors are blended, stirring once or twice during cooking time. Serve barbecue mixture in hamburger buns.

Total Cooking Time: 13 to 18 minutes

Wild Rice & Bacon Burgers

6 slices bacon
1 lb. ground beef, crumbled
¾ cup cooked wild rice
1 large egg
½ teaspoon seasoned salt

4 servings

1 Layer 3 paper towels on a plate. Arrange the bacon slices on the paper towels and cover with another paper towel. Microwave bacon at High for 3 to 7 minutes, or until crisp and golden brown. Crumble the bacon.

2 Combine the bacon and remaining ingredients in a medium bowl. Divide the mixture into 4 equal portions and shape each portion into a 4-inch round patty.

3 Arrange the patties on a roasting rack. Microwave at High for 4½ to 8 minutes, or until the meat is firm and no longer pink, turning burgers over once during cooking time. Let burgers stand, covered with wax paper, for 2 minutes before serving.

Total Cooking Time: 7½ to 15 minutes

Chili Burgers ▲

1 lb. ground beef, crumbled
½ cup chopped celery
½ cup chopped onion
½ cup chopped green pepper
1 can (15 oz.) chili with beans
½ cup catsup
1 teaspoon chili powder
½ teaspoon dry mustard
½ teaspoon salt
⅛ teaspoon cayenne
⅛ teaspoon pepper
⅛ teaspoon garlic powder

4 to 6 servings

1 In a 2-quart casserole combine the ground beef, celery, onion and green pepper. Cover; microwave at High for 5 to 8 minutes, or until the meat is no longer pink and the vegetables are tender-crisp, stirring once during cooking time. Drain.

2 Add the remaining ingredients, stirring to combine. Re-cover; microwave at High for 5 to 8 minutes, or until the mixture is hot and flavors are blended, stirring once during cooking time. Serve chili mixture in hamburger buns.

Total Cooking Time: 10 to 16 minutes

Meatball Hoagie

Meatballs:

- 1 lb. ground beef, crumbled
- 3 tablespoons taco sauce
- 2 tablespoons finely chopped onion
- 1 teaspoon chili powder
- ½ teaspoon salt
- ¼ teaspoon pepper
- ⅛ teaspoon garlic powder
- ⅛ teaspoon ground cinnamon

- ⅔ cup taco sauce
- ¾ cup shredded zucchini
- ¼ cup chopped green pepper
- 2 tablespoons chopped onion
- 4 hot dog buns, split

4 servings

1 Combine all the meatball ingredients in a medium bowl. Shape the mixture into 16 meatballs and arrange in a 2-quart casserole.

2 Microwave at High for 6 to 9 minutes, or until the meatballs are firm and no longer pink in the center, stirring gently to rearrange 3 or 4 times during cooking. Drain.

3 Pour ⅔ cup taco sauce over the meatballs. Cover; microwave at 50% (Medium) for 2 to 3 minutes, or until the meatballs and sauce are hot, stirring once during cooking time.

4 Combine zucchini, green pepper and onion in a small bowl. Spoon the mixture evenly into the hot dog buns. Arrange 4 meatballs in each bun, then spoon sauce over the meatballs.

Total Cooking Time: 8 to 12 minutes

Variation:

Italian Meatball Sandwich:
Follow recipe for Meatball Hoagie, except: substitute ½ teaspoon Italian seasoning for the chili powder and spaghetti sauce for the taco sauce; omit the cinnamon.

Mexican Pizza (pictured on pages 8-9)

1 tablespoon vegetable oil
2 flour tortillas (8-inch diameter)
½ lb. ground beef, crumbled
½ cup chopped onion
½ teaspoon chili powder
¼ teaspoon dried oregano leaves
¼ teaspoon ground cumin
¼ teaspoon garlic salt
1 medium tomato, seeded and chopped
½ cup chopped green pepper
1 cup shredded Monterey Jack cheese
1 cup shredded Cheddar cheese

2 to 4 servings

1 Heat oil conventionally in a 9-inch skillet over medium-high heat. Brown both sides of each tortilla in hot oil; remove from heat and set aside.

2 In a 1-quart casserole, microwave the ground beef and onion at High for 2 to 4 minutes, or until meat is no longer pink, stirring to break apart once or twice during cooking time. Drain.

3 Stir in the seasonings. Microwave at 50% (Medium) for 2 to 3 minutes, or until the flavors are blended, stirring once during cooking time. Stir in the tomato.

4 Place 1 tortilla on a serving plate. Top with half the meat mixture, half the green pepper and half of each of the cheeses. Microwave at High for 2 to 3 minutes, or until the cheese melts. Repeat with the remaining tortilla. If desired, serve pizzas with sour cream, salsa sauce, and guacamole.

Total Cooking Time: 8 to 13 minutes

Beef & Bean Burritos ▲

½ lb. ground beef, crumbled
¼ cup chopped onion
1 can (10½ oz.) bean dip
2 tablespoons taco, salsa or tomato sauce
½ teaspoon ground cumin
½ teaspoon dried oregano leaves
4 flour tortillas (10-inch diameter) softened according to pkg. directions
1 cup shredded Cheddar cheese

2 to 4 servings

1 Combine ground beef and onion in a 1-quart casserole. Microwave at High for 2 to 4 minutes, or until the meat is no longer pink, stirring to break apart once during cooking time. Drain.

2 Stir in the bean dip, taco sauce, cumin and oregano. Microwave at High for 3 to 4 minutes, or until the mixture is hot, stirring once during cooking time.

3 Divide meat mixture into 4 portions and spoon 1 portion down the center of each tortilla. Sprinkle evenly with the cheese. Fold in the sides and roll up each tortilla to enclose the filling.

4 Arrange 2 burritos on a plate. Microwave at High for 1 to 2 minutes, or until burritos are hot. Repeat with remaining burritos. If desired, top burritos with sour cream, shredded lettuce, chopped tomato and onion.

Total Cooking Time: 7 to 12 minutes

Tostadas

1 can (8 oz.) kidney beans, undrained
¼ cup chopped onion, divided
1 tablespoon water
¼ teaspoon ground cumin, divided
¼ teaspoon salt, divided
  Dash pepper
¼ lb. ground beef, crumbled
½ teaspoon chili powder
  Dash garlic powder
  Dash cayenne
2 tostada shells

Toppings:

½ cup shredded Monterey Jack or
    Cheddar cheese
½ cup shredded lettuce
¼ cup chopped green pepper
1 medium tomato, seeded and chopped
2 tablespoons chopped black olives
  Sour cream

2 servings

Follow photo directions, right.

Total Cooking Time: 8½ to 13¾ minutes

How to Microwave Tostadas

1 In a 1-quart casserole, combine the beans, 1 tablespoon of the onion, the water, ⅛ teaspoon each of cumin and salt, and the pepper. Cover; microwave at High for 6 to 8 minutes, or until beans mash easily, stirring twice during cooking time. Microwave for 1 to 2 minutes longer, or until excess liquid is absorbed. Set aside.

2 In a small bowl, combine the ground beef and the remaining onion, cumin and salt. Mix in the chili powder, garlic powder and cayenne. Microwave at High for 1 to 3 minutes, or until the meat is no longer pink, stirring to break apart once during cooking time. Drain; set aside.

3 On a paper-towel-lined plate, microwave the tostada shells at High for 30 to 45 seconds, or until hot to the touch. Spread half of the bean mixture on each shell, then top evenly with the meat mixture. Sprinkle tostadas with one or more of the toppings before serving.

Soups & Stews

Hot, hearty and complete:
main-course soups and stews
—ready in just minutes

◄ Hearty Winter Soup

    1 lb. ground beef, crumbled
    1 small onion, thinly sliced
    ⅓ cup chopped celery
    2½ cups hot tap water
    2 cups cubed potatoes (½-inch cubes)
    1 can (10½ oz.) condensed beef broth
    1 cup cubed rutabaga (½-inch cubes)
    1 cup coarsely chopped cabbage
    1 medium carrot, thinly sliced
    1 teaspoon seasoned salt
    ½ teaspoon dried rosemary leaves, crushed
    ⅛ teaspoon pepper

4 to 6 servings

1 Combine ground beef, onion and celery in a 3-quart casserole. Microwave at High for 4 to 7 minutes, or until meat is no longer pink, stirring to break apart once during cooking time. Drain.

2 Stir in the remaining ingredients. Cover, and microwave at High for 20 to 30 minutes, or until the vegetables are tender and the mixture is hot, stirring once or twice during cooking time. Let soup stand for 5 minutes before serving.

Total Cooking Time: 24 to 37 minutes

Soup Tip:
Prepare soups in large quantities and freeze in individual serving-size portions for later use. Defrost and reheat at High power, stirring occasionally to break apart.

Hamburger-Vegetable Soup ▲

    1 lb. lean ground beef, crumbled
    1 potato (8 to 10 oz.) cut into ¼-inch cubes
    1½ cups shredded cabbage
    3 cups hot tap water
    1 can (16 oz.) whole tomatoes
    1 pkg. (10 oz.) frozen mixed vegetables
    1 tablespoon instant beef bouillon granules
    1 tablespoon dried minced onion
    1 tablespoon dried parsley flakes
    1 teaspoon Worcestershire sauce
    ½ teaspoon salt

4 servings

1 Combine the ground beef, potato and cabbage in a 3-quart casserole. Cover; microwave at High for 4 to 7 minutes, or until the meat is no longer pink and the vegetables are tender-crisp, stirring once during cooking time.

2 Add the remaining ingredients. Cover, and microwave at High for 15 to 20 minutes, or until the vegetables are tender and mixture is hot, stirring once during cooking time.

Total Cooking Time: 19 to 27 minutes

Beefy Spaghetti Soup ▲

- 1 lb. ground beef, crumbled
- 1 medium onion, chopped
- ½ cup chopped celery
- 2 cups hot tap water
- 1½ cups uncooked broken spaghetti
- 1 can (10½ oz.) condensed beef consommé
- 1 can (8 oz.) tomato sauce
- 1 cup frozen cut green beans
- 1 can (4 oz.) sliced mushrooms, drained
- 1 teaspoon dried parsley flakes
- ¾ teaspoon salt
- ½ teaspoon Italian seasoning
- ⅛ teaspoon garlic powder
- ⅛ teaspoon pepper

4 to 6 servings

1 Combine ground beef, onion and celery in a 3-quart casserole. Microwave at High for 4 to 7 minutes, or until meat is no longer pink, stirring to break apart once during cooking time. Drain.

2 Stir in the remaining ingredients. Cover, and microwave at High for 18 to 25 minutes, or until the spaghetti is tender and the mixture is hot, stirring once or twice during cooking time. Let soup stand for 5 minutes before serving.

Total Cooking Time: 22 to 32 minutes

Tomato, Hamburger & Rice Soup

- ½ lb. ground beef, crumbled
- 3 tablespoons all-purpose flour
- 2 cups tomato juice
- ½ cup uncooked instant rice
- 1 tablespoon sugar
- 1 teaspoon salt
- ¼ teaspoon onion powder
- ⅛ teaspoon pepper
- 1½ cups milk

4 servings

1 In a 2-quart casserole, microwave the ground beef at High for 2 to 4 minutes, or until meat is no longer pink, stirring to break apart once during cooking time. Drain.

2 Stir in the flour. Add the tomato juice, rice, sugar and seasonings. Stir to combine. Cover; microwave at High for 5 to 6 minutes, or until the rice is tender and mixture is slightly thickened, stirring twice during cooking time.

3 Slowly blend in the milk. Microwave at High for 3 to 5 minutes, or until mixture is hot, stirring once during cooking time.

Total Cooking Time: 10 to 15 minutes

Hamburger & Bean Soup

  1 lb. ground beef, crumbled
⅔ cup chopped celery
⅔ cup chopped onion
  2 cups hot tap water
  1 can (16 oz.) whole tomatoes
  1 can (15½ oz.) cut wax beans
  1 can (10½ oz.) condensed beef broth
  1 pkg. (9 oz.) frozen cut green beans
  1 can (4 oz.) sliced mushrooms, drained
1½ teaspoons Worcestershire sauce
1½ teaspoons salt
  1 teaspoon Italian seasoning
  1 teaspoon dried parsley flakes

4 to 6 servings

1 Combine the ground beef, celery and onion in a 3-quart casserole. Microwave at High for 4 to 7 minutes, or until meat is no longer pink, stirring to break apart once during cooking time. Drain.

2 Stir in the remaining ingredients. Cover, and microwave at High for 15 to 20 minutes, or until the flavors are blended and mixture is hot, stirring once or twice during cooking time. Let soup stand for 5 minutes before serving.

Total Cooking Time: 19 to 27 minutes

Quick Hamburger & Vegetable Soup

½ lb. ground beef, crumbled
1⅔ cups hot tap water
  1 can (10½ oz.) condensed French onion soup
  1 large tomato, chopped
  1 can (4 oz.) sliced mushrooms, drained
⅓ cup frozen corn
⅓ cup frozen peas
½ teaspoon dried parsley flakes
¼ teaspoon dried marjoram leaves
⅛ teaspoon salt
⅛ teaspoon pepper

4 servings

1 In a 2-quart casserole, microwave the ground beef at High for 2 to 4 minutes, or until meat is no longer pink, stirring to break apart once during cooking time. Drain.

2 Stir in the remaining ingredients. Cover, and microwave at High for 10 to 15 minutes, or until the flavors are blended and the mixture is hot, stirring 2 or 3 times during cooking.

Total Cooking Time: 12 to 19 minutes

Italian Hamburger & Vegetable Soup

½ lb. ground beef, crumbled
  4 cups hot tap water
  1 can (8 oz.) tomato sauce
½ cup uncooked elbow macaroni
  1 pkg. (1.4 oz.) vegetable soup and recipe mix
  1 teaspoon sugar
¼ teaspoon Italian seasoning

4 servings

1 In a 3-quart casserole, microwave the ground beef at High for 2 to 4 minutes, or until the meat is no longer pink, stirring to break apart once during cooking time. Drain.

2 Stir in the remaining ingredients. Cover, and microwave at High for 17 to 20 minutes, or until the macaroni is tender, stirring twice during cooking time.

Total Cooking Time: 19 to 24 minutes

Creamy Beef & Sausage Soup

1 medium onion, thinly sliced
1 stalk celery, thinly sliced
1 cup thinly sliced carrots
½ lb. ground beef, crumbled
½ lb. bulk pork sausage, crumbled
2 cups hot tap water
1 can (16 oz.) Great Northern beans
1 can (10¾ oz.) condensed cream of
   celery soup
1 pkg. (9 oz.) frozen cut green beans
1 teaspoon salt
1 teaspoon dried parsley flakes
½ teaspoon dried basil leaves

4 servings

Follow photo directions, right.

Total Cooking Time: 23 to 33 minutes

Variation:

Creamy Beef, Sausage & Potato Soup:
Follow recipe for Creamy Beef & Sausage Soup,
except: substitute 1 can (10¾ oz.) condensed
cream of potato soup for cream of celery soup.

How to Microwave
Creamy Beef & Sausage Soup

1 Combine the onion, celery and carrots in a
3-quart casserole. Cover; microwave at High
for 4 to 6 minutes, or until vegetables are tender.

2 Add the ground beef and sausage. Microwave at High for 4 to 7 minutes, or until the meat is no longer pink, stirring to break apart once during cooking time. Drain.

3 Stir in the remaining ingredients. Cover, and microwave at High for 15 to 20 minutes, or until flavors are blended and mixture is hot.

◄ Chili

1 medium onion, thinly sliced
1 cup chopped celery
1 lb. ground beef, crumbled
2 cans (10¾ oz. each) condensed tomato soup
1 can (16 oz.) kidney beans
1 tablespoon chili powder
1 teaspoon Worcestershire sauce
½ teaspoon salt
⅛ teaspoon cayenne

4 to 6 servings

1 Combine the onion and celery in a 3-quart casserole. Cover; microwave at High for 4 to 6 minutes, or until the vegetables are tender, stirring once during cooking time.

2 Stir in the ground beef. Microwave at High for 4 to 7 minutes, or until the meat is no longer pink, stirring to break apart once during cooking time. Drain.

3 Stir in the remaining ingredients. Microwave at 50% (Medium) for 20 to 30 minutes, or until the flavors are blended and the mixture is hot, stirring once or twice during cooking time.

Total Cooking Time: 28 to 43 minutes

Italian Chili (pictured on pages 24-25)

½ lb. lean ground beef, crumbled
1 medium onion, chopped
½ cup chopped green pepper
½ cup chopped celery
⅛ teaspoon garlic powder
1 can (28 oz.) whole tomatoes, cut up
1 can (15 oz.) kidney beans, drained
1 can (12 oz.) tomato juice
1 can (8 oz.) sliced mushrooms, drained
1 can (6 oz.) tomato paste
1 pkg. (3½ oz.) sliced pepperoni, chopped
1½ teaspoons Italian seasoning
½ teaspoon salt
½ teaspoon sugar
¼ to ½ teaspoon crushed red pepper flakes

8 to 10 servings

Meatball Stew

1 lb. lean ground beef
1¾ cups beef broth
1 can (10¾ oz.) condensed tomato soup
1 pkg. (10 oz.) frozen mixed vegetables
1 medium onion, chopped
1 cup water
1 cup shredded cabbage
½ cup uncooked long grain rice
½ cup uncooked medium pearl barley
½ cup chopped celery
1 tablespoon dried parsley flakes
½ teaspoon salt
¼ teaspoon pepper

6 to 8 servings

1 Shape the ground beef into 18 meatballs. Set aside. In a 3-quart casserole, combine the remaining ingredients; mix well. Stir in the meatballs. Cover; microwave at High for 10 minutes. Stir gently.

2 Microwave at 70% (Medium High) for 20 to 30 minutes longer, or until the rice and barley are tender, stirring 2 or 3 times during cooking. Let stew stand for 5 minutes before serving.

Total Cooking Time: 30 to 40 minutes

1 In a 3-quart casserole, combine the ground beef, onion, green pepper, celery and garlic powder. Cover; microwave at High for 5 to 8 minutes, or until the meat is no longer pink and the vegetables are tender-crisp, stirring to break apart once or twice during cooking time. Stir in the remaining ingredients; re-cover.

2 Microwave the mixture at High for 20 minutes, stirring once during cooking time. Microwave, uncovered, at High for 10 to 15 minutes longer, or until chili reaches desired consistency and flavors are blended.

Total Cooking Time: 35 to 43 minutes

◄ Cajun Hamburger Stew

- 1 large onion, chopped
- 1 small canned or fresh jalapeño pepper, thinly sliced (optional)
- ⅛ teaspoon garlic powder
- 1 lb. ground beef, crumbled
- 1 can (16 oz.) stewed tomatoes
- 1 cup frozen mixed vegetables
- 1 cup water
- 1 pkg. (6 oz.) frozen sliced okra
- ½ cup cubed, fully cooked ham (½-inch cubes)
- 1 tablespoon chili powder
- 1 teaspoon salt
- 2 cans (16 oz. each) black-eyed peas, drained

8 to 10 servings

1 Combine onion, jalapeño slices and the garlic powder in a 3-quart casserole. Cover; microwave at High for 4 to 5 minutes, or until onion is tender, stirring once during cooking time.

2 Add the ground beef. Microwave at High for 4 to 7 minutes, or until the meat is no longer pink, stirring to break apart once during cooking time. Drain.

3 Stir in the remaining ingredients, except the peas. Cover; microwave at High for 15 to 20 minutes, or until the flavors are blended and the mixture is hot, stirring twice during cooking time.

4 Stir in the peas. Re-cover; microwave at High for 2 to 3 minutes, or until the mixture is hot. If desired, serve stew over hot cooked rice.

Total Cooking Time: 25 to 35 minutes

Zucchini Stew ▼

- 1 lb. ground beef, crumbled
- 1 pkg. (12 oz.) bulk pork sausage
- 1 medium green pepper, cut into thin strips
- 1 medium onion, thinly sliced
- 1 medium zucchini, thinly sliced
- 1 can (16 oz.) whole tomatoes
- 1 can (12 oz.) tomato juice
- 1 can (4 oz.) sliced mushrooms, drained
- 1 teaspoon seasoned salt
- ½ teaspoon dried oregano leaves
- ¼ teaspoon pepper
- ¼ teaspoon garlic powder

4 to 6 servings

1 In a 3-quart casserole, combine the ground beef, sausage, green pepper and onion. Cover; microwave at High for 8 to 12 minutes, or until the meat is no longer pink and the vegetables are tender, stirring to break apart 2 or 3 times during cooking. Drain.

2 Stir in the remaining ingredients. Cover, and microwave at High for 15 to 20 minutes, or until the flavors are blended and the mixture is hot, stirring once or twice during cooking time. Let stew stand for 5 minutes. If desired, sprinkle with Parmesan cheese before serving.

Total Cooking Time: 23 to 32 minutes

Stuffed Pepper Stew

3 cups hot tap water
¾ lb. beef stew meat, cut into ½-inch pieces
1 can (8 oz.) whole tomatoes, cut up
1 cup thinly sliced carrots
½ cup thinly sliced celery
½ cup chopped onion
1 tablespoon instant beef bouillon granules
1 teaspoon salt, divided

½ teaspoon pepper, divided
½ teaspoon dried parsley flakes
4 medium green peppers
½ lb. lean ground beef, crumbled
⅔ cup uncooked instant rice

4 servings

Follow photo directions, below.

Total Cooking Time: 65 to 95 minutes

How to Microwave Stuffed Pepper Stew

1 In a 3-quart casserole, combine the water, stew meat, tomatoes, carrots, celery, onion, bouillon, ½ teaspoon of the salt, ¼ teaspoon of the pepper, and the parsley. Cover; microwave at High for 5 minutes. Microwave at 50% (Medium) for 30 minutes longer. Set aside.

2 Cut a ½-inch slice from the top of each pepper. Remove and discard seeds; reserve tops of peppers. Remove a thin slice from the bottom of each pepper; stand peppers upright.

3 In a small bowl, combine the ground beef, rice and the remaining salt and pepper. Stuff peppers loosely with the ground beef mixture.

4 Stir the soup. Arrange stuffed peppers upright in soup; top peppers with reserved pepper tops. Cover; microwave at 50% (Medium) for 30 to 60 minutes, or until the stew meat is tender, rotating casserole once or twice during cooking time. Serve stew in soup bowls.

Sauces & Toppings

Create a special crowning touch using ingredients you have on hand

Pizza Potato Topper

 4 baking potatoes (8 to 10 oz. each)
½ lb. ground beef, crumbled
½ cup chopped onion
½ cup chopped green pepper
 1 cup seeded chopped tomato
¼ cup catsup
½ teaspoon Italian seasoning
¼ teaspoon salt
　 Dash cayenne
½ cup shredded mozzarella cheese

4 servings

Follow photo directions, right.

Total Cooking Time: 16 to 26 minutes

How to Microwave Pizza Potato Topper

1 Prick potatoes with a fork. Wrap each potato in a paper towel. Microwave at High for 10 to 16 minutes, or until the potatoes are just soft to the touch, turning over once during cooking time. Wrap each potato in foil; set aside.

2 Place ground beef, onion and green pepper in a 2-quart casserole. Cover, and microwave at High for 3 to 6 minutes, or until the meat is no longer pink and vegetables are tender, stirring 2 or 3 times during cooking. Drain. Add chopped tomato, catsup and seasonings.

3 Unwrap potatoes and split open; arrange on a serving plate. Divide meat mixture into 4 portions and spoon 1 portion into center of each potato. Sprinkle evenly with cheese; microwave at High for 3 to 4 minutes, or until cheese melts, rotating dish once during cooking time.

41

Beefy Mushroom Potato Topper

4 baking potatoes (8 to 10 oz. each)
½ lb. ground beef, crumbled
2 cups sliced fresh mushrooms
1 small onion, thinly sliced
⅛ teaspoon instant minced garlic
1 pkg. (.87 oz.) brown gravy mix
¾ cup water
1 teaspoon dried parsley flakes

4 servings

1 Prick potatoes with a fork. Wrap each potato in a paper towel. Microwave at High for 10 to 16 minutes, or until potatoes are just soft to the touch, turning over once during cooking time. Wrap each potato in foil; set aside.

2 Place the ground beef, mushrooms, onion and garlic in a 2-quart casserole. Cover, and microwave at High for 7 to 9 minutes, or until the meat is no longer pink and the vegetables are tender, stirring to break apart once or twice during cooking time. Drain.

3 Stir in the remaining ingredients. Microwave at High for 6 to 7 minutes, or until the mixture is thickened and hot, stirring once or twice during cooking time.

4 Unwrap potatoes and split open. Divide meat mixture into 4 portions and spoon 1 portion into the center of each potato.

Total Cooking Time: 23 to 32 minutes

Taco Potatoes (pictured on pages 38-39)

4 baking potatoes (8 to 10 oz. each)
1 lb. ground beef, crumbled
1 pkg. (1.25 oz.) chili seasoning mix
1 can (8 oz.) tomato sauce
¼ cup sour cream
½ cup shredded Cheddar cheese
¼ cup sliced green onions

4 servings

1 Prick potatoes with a fork. Wrap each in a paper towel. Microwave at High for 10 to 16 minutes, or until the potatoes are just soft to the touch, turning over once during cooking time. Wrap each potato in foil; set aside.

2 In a 2-quart casserole, microwave the ground beef at High for 4 to 7 minutes, or until the meat is no longer pink, stirring to break apart once or twice during cooking time. Drain.

3 Add the chili seasoning mix and tomato sauce. Stir to combine. Cover; microwave at High for 3 to 4 minutes, or until mixture is hot. Unwrap potatoes and split open; arrange on serving plate.

4 Place 1 tablespoon of the sour cream in the center of each potato. Divide meat mixture into 4 portions and spoon 1 portion into the center of each potato. Sprinkle evenly with the cheese and green onions. Microwave at High for 2 to 3 minutes, or until the cheese melts, rotating dish once during cooking time.

Total Cooking Time: 19 to 30 minutes

Picadillo ▲

½ cup chopped onion
⅓ cup chopped green pepper
1 tablespoon olive or vegetable oil
¼ teaspoon instant minced garlic
1 lb. ground beef, crumbled
1 can (16 oz.) whole tomatoes, cut up
1 can (6 oz.) tomato paste
½ cup hot tap water
⅓ cup raisins
2 tablespoons capers (optional)
1 tablespoon red wine vinegar
2 teaspoons packed brown sugar
1 teaspoon dried oregano leaves
½ teaspoon salt

4 to 6 servings

1 In a 2-quart casserole, combine the onion, green pepper, olive oil and garlic. Cover; microwave at High for 2 to 4 minutes, or until vegetables are tender, stirring once during cooking time.

2 Add the ground beef. Microwave at High for 4 to 7 minutes, or until meat is no longer pink, stirring to break apart once or twice during cooking time. Drain.

3 Stir in the remaining ingredients. Microwave at High for 8 to 10 minutes, or until the mixture is hot and the flavors are blended, stirring once or twice during cooking time. Serve picadillo over hot cooked rice.

Total Cooking Time: 14 to 21 minutes

◄ Coney Island Sauce

   1 lb. ground beef, crumbled
  ½ cup chopped onion
   1 can (8 oz.) tomato sauce
  ¼ cup catsup
 1½ teaspoons chili powder
  ½ teaspoon cayenne
  ½ teaspoon salt
  ¼ teaspoon pepper

2 cups

1 In a 2-quart casserole, microwave the ground beef and onion at High for 4 to 7 minutes, or until the meat is no longer pink, stirring to break apart once or twice during cooking time. Drain.

2 Add the remaining ingredients. Microwave at High for 6 to 10 minutes, or until the mixture is hot and the flavors are blended, stirring once or twice during cooking time. Serve sauce as a topping for hot dogs or Polish sausages.

Total Cooking Time: 10 to 17 minutes

Hamburger Stroganoff

   1 lb. ground beef, crumbled
   2 teaspoons instant minced onion
   1 can (10¾ oz.) condensed cream of
      mushroom soup
 ¾ cup milk
   1 can (4 oz.) sliced mushrooms, drained
   1 teaspoon Worcestershire sauce
  ½ teaspoon garlic salt
  ½ cup sour cream

4 to 6 servings

1 In a 2-quart casserole, microwave the ground beef and onion at High for 4 to 7 minutes, or until meat is no longer pink, stirring to break apart once or twice during cooking time. Drain.

2 Add the remaining ingredients, except sour cream. Mix well. Cover; microwave at High for 6 to 8 minutes, or until the mixture is hot and bubbly, stirring once during cooking time.

3 Stir in the sour cream. Re-cover; microwave at High for 1 to 2 minutes, or until mixture is hot. If desired, serve over noodles or hot cooked rice.

Total Cooking Time: 11 to 17 minutes

Italian Meat Sauce

1 cup chopped onion
½ cup chopped green pepper
1 tablespoon olive or vegetable oil
1 lb. ground beef, crumbled
1 lb. bulk Italian sausage, crumbled
2 cans (16 oz. each) tomato sauce
1 can (16 oz.) whole tomatoes, cut up
1 can (6 oz.) tomato paste
2 teaspoons Italian seasoning
2 teaspoons sugar
1 teaspoon salt
⅛ teaspoon garlic powder

2 quarts

1 In a 3-quart casserole, place the onion, green pepper and olive oil. Cover; microwave at High for 3 to 6 minutes, or until vegetables are tender, stirring once during cooking time.

2 Add the ground beef and Italian sausage. Mix well. Microwave at High for 6 to 11 minutes, or until the meat is no longer pink, stirring to break apart once or twice during cooking time. Drain.

3 Add remaining ingredients, stirring to combine. Microwave at High for 7 to 15 minutes, or until the mixture is hot and flavors are blended. If desired, serve sauce with hot cooked noodles. (Or freeze in containers for future use. Defrost frozen sauce as directed in chart, below.)

Total Cooking Time: 16 to 32 minutes

Servings:	Casserole Size:	Microwave Time at High:
2 (1½ cups)	1 qt.	6-10 minutes
4 (3 cups)	1-1½ qt.	12-17 minutes

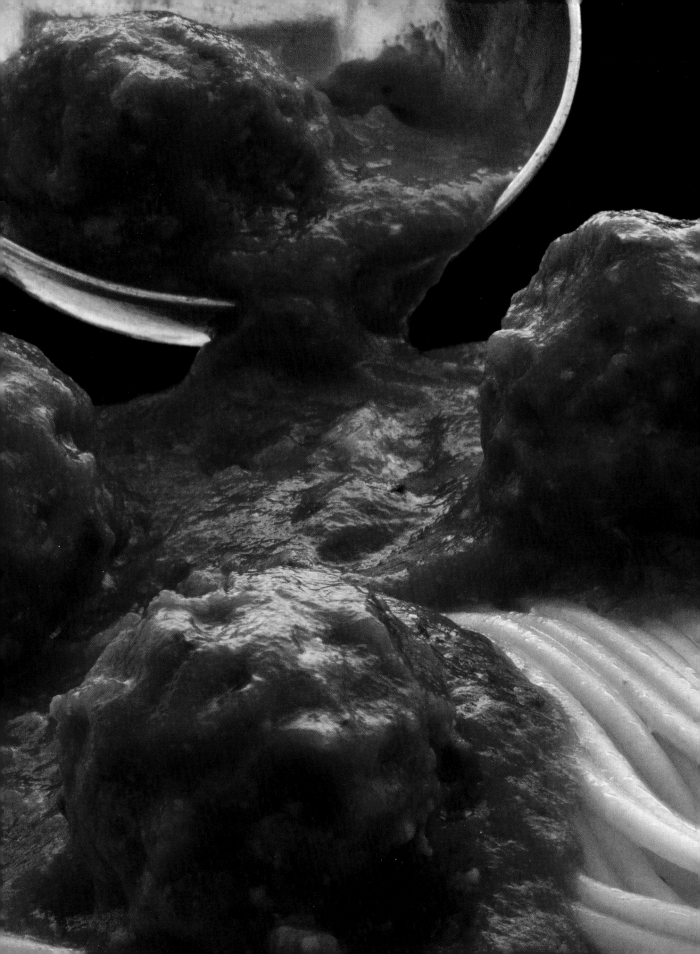

Meatballs

Meatballs

*Versatile and easy — great
as an appetizer or main course*

Traditional Meatballs

Meatballs:
1 lb. ground beef, crumbled
1 cup soft bread crumbs
1 large egg
¼ cup chopped onion
¼ cup chopped green pepper
2 tablespoons milk
1 teaspoon dried parsley flakes
¼ teaspoon salt
⅛ teaspoon pepper

Sauce:
1 pkg. (.87 oz.) onion gravy mix
1 cup cold water

12 meatballs

1 Combine all the meatball ingredients in a medium bowl. Shape mixture into 12 meatballs and arrange in a 9-inch square baking dish. Microwave at High for 6 to 9 minutes, or until the meatballs are firm and no longer pink in the center, stirring gently to rearrange 2 or 3 times during cooking. Drain. Cover and set aside.

2 Combine the gravy mix and water in a 4-cup measure. Microwave at High for 1 to 3 minutes, or until the mixture thickens and bubbles, stirring 2 or 3 times during cooking. Pour sauce over meatballs; toss to coat. If desired, serve sauce and meatballs over parslied rice.

Total Cooking Time: 7 to 12 minutes

Meatballs & Tomato Sauce
(pictured on pages 46-47)

Meatballs:
1 lb. ground beef, crumbled
¼ lb. ground pork, crumbled
½ cup uncooked quick-cooking rolled oats
¼ cup grated Parmesan cheese
¼ cup milk
1 large egg, beaten
½ teaspoon salt
⅛ teaspoon garlic powder (optional)
3 tablespoons olive or vegetable oil

Sauce:
¾ cup chopped onion
⅓ cup chopped celery (optional)
2 cans (16 oz. each) tomato sauce
1 can (16 oz.) whole tomatoes
1 can (6 oz.) tomato paste
1 tablespoon dried parsley flakes (optional)
1 tablespoon packed brown sugar
1 tablespoon Italian seasoning
½ teaspoon chili powder (optional)

6 to 8 servings

1 Combine all the meatball ingredients, except olive oil, in a medium bowl. Shape mixture into 36 meatballs.

2 Heat olive oil conventionally in a large skillet over medium-high heat. Add meatballs; brown for about 5 minutes, turning meatballs during cooking. Remove meatballs from heat and drain, reserving 2 tablespoons of drippings. Set aside.

3 Place reserved drippings in a 3-quart casserole. Add the onion and celery. Cover; microwave at High for 3 to 6 minutes, or until vegetables are tender. Stir in the remaining sauce ingredients and the meatballs. Re-cover.

4 Microwave at High for 10 minutes. Stir, and microwave at 70% (Medium High) for 20 to 30 minutes longer, or until the flavors are blended, stirring 2 or 3 times during cooking. Serve meatballs over hot cooked spaghetti noodles.

Total Cooking Time: 38 to 51 minutes

Rigatoni & Meatballs

Sauce:

1 can (16 oz.) whole tomatoes,
    drained and cut up
1 jar (15½ oz.) spaghetti sauce
½ teaspoon Italian seasoning

Meatballs:

1 lb. lean ground beef, crumbled
1 large egg
2 tablespoons grated Parmesan cheese
2 tablespoons seasoned dry bread crumbs
¾ teaspoon Italian seasoning
¼ teaspoon salt
⅛ teaspoon garlic powder

8 oz. uncooked rigatoni, prepared as directed
    on pkg.
1 cup shredded mozzarella cheese

4 servings

1 Combine all the sauce ingredients in a 2-quart casserole; set aside. Combine all the meatball ingredients in a medium bowl; shape mixture into 12 meatballs.

2 Add the meatballs to the sauce mixture, stirring gently to coat. Cover; microwave at High for 10 to 16 minutes, or until the meatballs are firm and no longer pink in the center, stirring gently to rearrange 2 or 3 times during cooking.

3 Stir in the cooked rigatoni and sprinkle with mozzarella cheese. Microwave at High for 2 to 4 minutes, or until the cheese melts, rotating casserole once during cooking time.

Total Cooking Time: 12 to 20 minutes

Meatballs with Tomato & Green Pepper Sauce

Meatballs:
 1 lb. ground beef, crumbled
 1 large egg
 ½ cup shredded carrot
 ¼ teaspoon salt

Sauce:
 4 medium tomatoes, seeded and chopped
 1 medium green pepper, cut into thin strips
 ¼ cup chopped onion
 1 tablespoon olive or vegetable oil
 ½ teaspoon garlic salt
 ½ teaspoon Italian seasoning
 1 tablespoon cornstarch
 1 tablespoon cold water

4 servings

1 Combine all the meatball ingredients in a medium bowl. Shape the mixture into 12 meatballs and place in a 9-inch square baking dish. Microwave at High for 6 to 9 minutes, or until the meatballs are firm and no longer pink in the center, stirring gently to rearrange 3 or 4 times during cooking. Drain. Cover; set aside.

2 In a 2-quart casserole, combine all the sauce ingredients, except the cornstarch and water. Set aside. Combine the cornstarch and water in a small bowl, stirring until dissolved. Add the cornstarch mixture to the sauce. Cover.

3 Microwave at High for 9 to 15 minutes, or until the green pepper is tender and the sauce is clear and slightly thickened, stirring 2 or 3 times during cooking. Add meatballs to the sauce. If desired, serve meatballs and sauce over hot cooked rice.

Total Cooking Time: 15 to 24 minutes

Swedish Meatballs

Meatballs:
  1 lb. ground beef, crumbled
  1 large egg
  ¼ cup chopped onion
  ¼ cup unseasoned dry bread crumbs
  ½ teaspoon seasoned salt
  ¼ teaspoon garlic powder
  ⅛ teaspoon ground nutmeg
  ⅛ teaspoon ground cinnamon
  ⅛ teaspoon pepper

Sauce:
  ⅓ cup butter or margarine
  ⅓ cup all-purpose flour
  ¼ teaspoon salt
  ¾ cup half-and-half
  ¾ cup chicken broth

4 servings

1 Combine all the meatball ingredients in a medium bowl. Shape mixture into 12 meatballs and place in a 2-quart casserole. Microwave at High for 6 to 9 minutes, or until the meatballs are firm and no longer pink in the center, stirring gently to rearrange 3 or 4 times during cooking. Drain. Cover; set aside.

2 In a 4-cup measure, microwave the butter at High for 1½ to 1¾ minutes, or until melted. Stir in the flour and salt, and blend in remaining sauce ingredients.

3 Microwave at High for 4 to 6 minutes, or until mixture thickens and bubbles, stirring after every minute of cooking time. Pour sauce over meatballs. (If necessary, microwave at High for 1 to 2 minutes longer to reheat.) If desired, serve meatballs with noodles or hot cooked rice and lightly sprinkle each serving with ground nutmeg.

Total Cooking Time: 11½ to 16¾ minutes

◄ Snappy Glazed Meatballs

Meatballs:
- 1 lb. ground beef, crumbled
- ¼ cup unseasoned dry bread crumbs
- ¼ cup chopped onion
- 1 large egg
- 1 teaspoon Worcestershire sauce
- ½ teaspoon salt

Sauce:
- 1 jar (10 oz.) apricot jam or pineapple preserves
- ½ cup chili sauce
- ¼ teaspoon chili powder

4 servings

1 Combine all the meatball ingredients in a medium bowl. Shape the mixture into 12 meatballs and place in a 2-quart casserole. Microwave at High for 6 to 9 minutes, or until the meatballs are firm and no longer pink in the center, stirring gently to rearrange once or twice during cooking time.

2 Combine sauce ingredients in a medium bowl. Pour mixture over meatballs, stirring gently to coat. Microwave at High for 2 to 4 minutes, or until mixture is hot, stirring once during cooking time. If desired, serve meatballs and sauce over hot cooked rice.

Total Cooking Time: 8 to 13 minutes

Middle Eastern Meatballs ►

Meatballs:
- 1 lb. lean ground beef, crumbled
- 1 small onion, finely chopped
- ½ teaspoon dried mint leaves
- ½ teaspoon dried parsley flakes
- ½ teaspoon salt
- ¼ teaspoon ground cinnamon
- ¼ teaspoon ground cumin

- 3 medium tomatoes, chopped
- 1 small onion, chopped
- ½ cup chopped green pepper
- 2 tablespoons dried parsley flakes
- 1 tablespoon olive or vegetable oil
- 1 teaspoon salt
- ¼ teaspoon garlic powder

4 servings

1 Combine all the meatball ingredients in a medium bowl. Shape the mixture into 12 meatballs and arrange in a 9-inch square baking dish.

2 Microwave at High for 6 to 9 minutes, or until the meatballs are firm and no longer pink in the center, stirring gently to rearrange once or twice during cooking time. Remove meatballs from dish; cover and set aside.

3 In the same dish, combine the remaining ingredients. Cover with plastic wrap; microwave at High for 4 to 6 minutes, or until the vegetables are tender, stirring once or twice during cooking time. Arrange the meatballs over the sauce. Serve meatballs and sauce over hot cooked rice.

Total Cooking Time: 10 to 15 minutes

Meatballs with Savory Rice ▲

- 1 lb. lean ground beef, crumbled
- ¾ cup chopped onion, divided
- ¼ cup unseasoned dry bread crumbs
- 1 large egg
- 3 tablespoons soy sauce, divided
- ½ teaspoon seasoned salt
- ½ cup chopped celery
- 2 cups uncooked instant rice
- 1 can (10¾ oz.) condensed cream of mushroom soup
- 1 cup water
- 1 can (4 oz.) sliced mushrooms, drained

4 servings

1 In a medium bowl, combine the ground beef, ¼ cup of the onion, the bread crumbs, egg, 1 tablespoon of the soy sauce and the seasoned salt. Shape the mixture into 20 meatballs and place in a 9-inch square baking dish.

2 Microwave at High for 8 to 10 minutes, or until the meatballs are firm and no longer pink in the center, stirring gently to rearrange 3 or 4 times during cooking. Remove meatballs from dish; cover and set aside.

3 In the same dish, place the celery and the remaining onion. Cover with plastic wrap; microwave at High for 4 to 6 minutes, or until the vegetables are tender, stirring once during cooking time.

4 Add the remaining soy sauce and remaining ingredients. Stir to combine. Re-cover; microwave at High for 4 to 6 minutes, or until the rice is tender, stirring once or twice during cooking time. (If necessary, microwave the meatballs for 1 to 2 minutes longer to reheat.) Arrange the meatballs over rice mixture to serve.

Total Cooking Time: 16 to 22 minutes

Meatballs with Creamy Herb Sauce

Meatballs:
- 1 lb. ground beef, crumbled
- ½ cup soft bread crumbs
- 1 large egg
- 2 tablespoons finely chopped onion
- ½ teaspoon salt
- ⅛ teaspoon pepper

Sauce:
- 2 tablespoons butter or margarine
- 1 tablespoon cornstarch
- 1 tablespoon dried parsley flakes
- ¼ teaspoon dried thyme leaves
- 1 can (5 oz.) evaporated milk
- ½ cup chicken broth

4 servings

1 Combine all the meatball ingredients in a medium bowl. Shape the mixture into 20 meatballs and place in a 9-inch square baking dish. Microwave at High for 8 to 10 minutes, or until the meatballs are firm and no longer pink in the center, stirring gently to rearrange 3 or 4 times during cooking. Drain. Cover meatballs and set aside.

2 In a 4-cup measure, microwave the butter at High for 45 seconds to 1 minute, or until melted. Add the cornstarch, parsley and thyme. Blend in the evaporated milk and chicken broth.

3 Microwave at High for 2½ to 4 minutes, or until the sauce thickens and bubbles, stirring 2 or 3 times during cooking. Pour sauce over meatballs. (If necessary, microwave at High for 1 to 2 minutes longer to reheat.) If desired, serve meatballs and sauce over hot buttered noodles.

Total Cooking Time: 11¼ to 15 minutes

Meatballs with Potatoes & Carrots

Meatballs:

- 1 lb. ground beef, crumbled
- ¼ cup unseasoned dry bread crumbs
- 1 large egg
- 1 teaspoon bouquet sauce
- ½ teaspoon salt
- ¼ teaspoon dry mustard (optional)
- ⅛ teaspoon garlic powder
- ⅛ teaspoon pepper

- 4 medium carrots, thinly sliced
- 1 potato (8 to 10 oz.) cut into ½-inch cubes
- 1 medium onion, thinly sliced
- 2 tablespoons water
- 1 tablespoon instant beef bouillon granules
- 2 teaspoons dried parsley flakes

4 servings

1 Combine all the meatball ingredients in a medium bowl. Shape the mixture into 20 meatballs; set aside.

2 Combine all the remaining ingredients in a 9-inch square baking dish. Cover with plastic wrap; microwave at High for 8 to 11 minutes, or until the vegetables are tender-crisp, stirring once or twice during cooking time.

3 Arrange meatballs over the vegetable mixture. Microwave at High for 9 to 11 minutes, or until the meatballs are firm and no longer pink in the center, rearranging 3 or 4 times during cooking.

Total Cooking Time: 17 to 22 minutes

Meatball Tip:
If you prefer darker colored meatballs, mix ½ teaspoon bouquet sauce or Worcestershire sauce into the meat mixture before shaping into meatballs.

Mediterranean Meatball Kabobs

4 wooden skewers (10 inches long)

Meatballs:

1 lb. ground beef, crumbled
3 tablespoons unseasoned dry bread crumbs
1 large egg
1 teaspoon dried parsley flakes
½ teaspoon dried mint leaves, crushed
¼ teaspoon dried rosemary leaves, crushed
¼ teaspoon pepper

2 small red potatoes (2½ inches) cut in half
1 medium red or green pepper, cut into 16 chunks
1 medium zucchini, cut into 8 chunks
2 tablespoons butter or margarine
¼ teaspoon garlic powder
1 teaspoon dried parsley flakes

4 servings

Follow photo directions, below.

Total Cooking Time: 15¾ to 19 minutes

How to Microwave Mediterranean Meatball Kabobs

1 Combine all the meatball ingredients in a medium bowl. Shape mixture into 12 meatballs. Set aside.

2 Assemble kabobs by placing ingredients on skewers in the following order: potato, red pepper, meatball, red pepper, zucchini, meatball, zucchini, red pepper, meatball and red pepper. Arrange kabobs on a roasting rack.

56

3 Place the butter, garlic powder and parsley in a 1-cup measure. Microwave at High for 45 seconds to 1 minute, or until butter melts. Brush kabobs with butter mixture. Cover with wax paper.

4 Microwave at High for 15 to 18 minutes, or until meatballs are firm and no longer pink in the center, rotating rack and rearranging kabobs twice during cooking time. If desired, serve kabobs with hot cooked rice or couscous.

Creamy Dill Meatballs

Meatballs:

1 lb. ground beef, crumbled
1 large egg
¼ cup chopped onion
¼ cup unseasoned dry bread crumbs
½ teaspoon salt
½ teaspoon dry mustard
¼ teaspoon garlic powder
⅛ teaspoon pepper

Sauce:

2 tablespoons butter or margarine
2 tablespoons all-purpose flour
½ teaspoon dried dill weed
½ teaspoon paprika, divided
¼ teaspoon salt
⅛ teaspoon pepper
1 cup milk

4 servings

1 Combine all the meatball ingredients in a medium bowl. Shape mixture into 20 meatballs and place in a 2-quart casserole. Microwave at High for 8 to 10 minutes, or until the meatballs are firm and no longer pink in the center, stirring gently to rearrange 3 or 4 times during cooking. Drain. Cover meatballs and set aside.

2 In a 4-cup measure, microwave butter at High for 45 seconds to 1 minute, or until melted. Stir in the flour, dill weed, ¼ teaspoon of the paprika, the salt and pepper. Blend in the milk.

3 Microwave at High for 3 to 5 minutes, or until mixture thickens and bubbles, stirring after every minute of cooking time.

4 Pour sauce over meatballs and sprinkle with remaining paprika. (If necessary, microwave at High for 1 to 2 minutes longer to reheat.) If desired, serve meatballs over hot buttered noodles.

Total Cooking Time: 11¾ to 16 minutes

Variation:

Creamy Herb Meatballs:
Follow recipe for Creamy Dill Meatballs, except: substitute ½ teaspoon dried marjoram, basil or summer savory leaves for the dill weed.

Sweet & Sour Meatballs

2 cans (8 oz. each) pineapple chunks, drained
  (reserve juice)
¾ cup packed brown sugar
¾ cup cider vinegar
¼ cup cornstarch
¼ cup soy sauce

Meatballs:

1 lb. ground beef, crumbled
1 large egg
¼ cup unseasoned dry bread crumbs
1 tablespoon soy sauce
1 green pepper, thinly sliced

4 to 6 servings

1 In a 2-cup measure, combine the reserved pineapple juice with enough water to equal 1⅓ cups; set aside. In a 2-quart casserole, combine the brown sugar, vinegar, cornstarch and soy sauce. Blend in the pineapple juice mixture. Microwave at High for 7 to 15 minutes, or until the mixture is clear and thickened, stirring 3 or 4 times during cooking. Set aside.

2 Combine all the meatball ingredients in a medium bowl. Shape the mixture into 20 meatballs. Arrange the meatballs in a 9-inch square baking dish and sprinkle evenly with green pepper slices.

3 Microwave at High for 8 to 10 minutes, or until the meatballs are firm and no longer pink in the center, stirring gently to rearrange once or twice during cooking time. Drain.

4 Add the meatballs, green pepper slices and pineapple chunks to the sauce. Microwave at High for 4 to 6 minutes, or until mixture is hot, stirring once or twice during cooking time. If desired, serve meatballs over hot cooked rice or chow mein noodles.

Total Cooking Time: 19 to 31 minutes

Meatloaf

Meatloaf

*From traditional to unexpected —
the last word on a quick & easy classic*

Traditional Meatloaf

1½ lbs. ground beef, crumbled
3 cups soft bread crumbs
2 large eggs
¼ cup milk
¼ cup chopped onion
1 tablespoon Worcestershire sauce
½ teaspoon salt
⅛ teaspoon pepper

4 to 6 servings

Follow photo directions, right.

Total Cooking Time: 13 to 18 minutes

How to Microwave Traditional Meatloaf

1 Combine all the ingredients in a medium bowl. Shape the mixture into a loaf and place in an 8 × 4-inch loaf dish.

2 Microwave at High for 13 to 18 minutes, or until the meatloaf is firm and temperature in center is 145°F, rotating dish once during cooking time.

3 Let the meatloaf stand, covered with wax paper, for 5 minutes before serving. If desired, garnish with catsup and parsley.

Bacon-wrapped Mini Meatloaves

½ cup chopped green pepper
½ cup chopped onion
4 slices bacon
1 lb. ground beef, crumbled
1 slice soft bread, cut into ½-inch cubes
1 large egg
2 tablespoons milk
2 tablespoons catsup
1 tablespoon Worcestershire sauce
½ teaspoon salt
⅛ teaspoon pepper

4 servings

1 Combine the green pepper and onion in a small bowl. Cover with plastic wrap, and microwave at High for 1½ to 3 minutes, or until the vegetables are tender-crisp. Set aside.

2 Layer 3 paper towels on a plate. Arrange the bacon slices on the paper towels and cover with another paper towel. Microwave at High for 2 to 3½ minutes, or just until bacon begins to brown. Set aside.

3 In a medium bowl, combine the ground beef, vegetable mixture, and the remaining ingredients. Divide the mixture into 2 equal portions and shape each portion into a 6 × 3½-inch loaf. Wrap 2 strips of bacon around each loaf; secure with wooden picks.

4 Place the loaves on a roasting rack. Microwave at High for 8 to 14 minutes, or until meatloaves are firm and no longer pink, rotating rack 2 or 3 times during cooking. Let meatloaves stand, covered, for 5 minutes before serving.

Total Cooking Time: 11½ to 20½ minutes

Wild Rice Stuffed Meatloaf

Meat Mixture:

1½ lbs. ground beef, crumbled
 1 can (10¾ oz.) condensed cream of
    mushroom soup, divided
 1 cup soft bread crumbs
 1 large egg
¼ cup chopped celery
 2 tablespoons chopped onion
 1 teaspoon Worcestershire sauce
⅛ teaspoon pepper

Filling:

 1 cup cooked wild or brown rice
 1 tablespoon grated Parmesan or
    Romano cheese
½ teaspoon dried marjoram leaves
⅛ teaspoon garlic powder

4 to 6 servings

1 Combine the ground beef and ½ cup of the condensed mushroom soup in a medium bowl. Add the remaining meatloaf ingredients; stir to combine. Press half of the meat mixture into the bottom of an 8 × 4-inch loaf dish. Make a slight indentation lengthwise down the center of the meat layer.

2 Combine the remaining mushroom soup and all the filling ingredients in a small bowl. Spoon the filling mixture lengthwise down the center of the meat layer. Top with the remaining meat mixture, and press to enclose filling and seal the edges.

3 Microwave at High for 13 to 18 minutes, or until the meatloaf is firm and the temperature in the center is 145°F, rotating dish once during cooking time. Let meatloaf stand, covered, for 5 minutes before serving.

Total Cooking Time: 13 to 18 minutes

Herb Meatloaf

Topping:
 2 tablespoons butter or margarine
 ⅓ cup seasoned dry bread crumbs
 ½ teaspoon dried parsley flakes

Meatloaf:
1½ lbs. ground beef, crumbled
 2 cups soft bread crumbs
 2 large eggs
 ⅓ cup red wine
 ¼ cup chopped onion
 1 tablespoon dried parsley flakes
 1 teaspoon dried bouquet garni seasoning
 ½ teaspoon salt
 ½ teaspoon instant beef bouillon granules

4 to 6 servings

1 In a small bowl, microwave the butter at High for 45 seconds to 1 minute, or until melted. Stir in remaining topping ingredients. Set aside.

2 Combine all the meatloaf ingredients in a medium bowl. Shape the mixture into a loaf and place in an 8 × 4-inch loaf dish. Microwave at High for 13 to 18 minutes, or until meatloaf is firm and temperature in the center is 145°F, rotating dish once during cooking time. Sprinkle with topping mixture. Let meatloaf stand, covered, for 5 minutes before serving.

Total Cooking Time: 13¾ to 19 minutes

Stuffed Meat Cups ▲

 1 pkg. (10 oz.) frozen chopped spinach
Meat Mixture:
 1 lb. ground beef, crumbled
 1 large egg
 ¼ cup unseasoned dry bread crumbs
 2 tablespoons catsup
 ½ teaspoon salt
 ¼ teaspoon pepper

 4 slices bacon
 1 cup shredded Swiss cheese

4 servings

Unwrap the spinach and place on a plate. Microwave spinach at High for 4 to 6 minutes, or until defrosted, turning over and breaking apart once during cooking time. Drain, pressing to remove excess moisture. Continue with photo directions, opposite.

Total Cooking Time: 16 to 27 minutes

Filling Variation:

Mushroom & Cheese Stuffed Meat Cups:
Follow recipe for Stuffed Meat Cups, except: Omit the spinach, bacon and Swiss cheese. In a small bowl, combine 1 can (4 oz.) sliced mushrooms (drained), 1 cup shredded Cheddar cheese and ½ cup sliced green onions. Stuff the meat cups as directed.

How to Microwave Stuffed Meat Cups

1 Combine all the meat mixture ingredients in a medium bowl. Set aside ⅓ of the mixture. Divide the remaining ⅔ of the mixture into 4 equal portions. Press each portion into a 6-oz. custard cup to form a shell. Set aside.

2 Layer 3 paper towels on a plate. Arrange the bacon on the paper towels and cover with another paper towel. Microwave at High for 3 to 6 minutes, or until bacon is crisp and golden brown. Crumble bacon.

3 Combine the spinach, bacon and Swiss cheese in a small bowl. Divide mixture into 4 portions and press 1 portion into the center of each meat cup. Shape remaining meat mixture into 4 patties; place patties over filled meat cups and press edges to seal.

4 Arrange the stuffed meat cups on a paper-towel-lined plate. Microwave at High for 9 to 15 minutes, or until the meat cups are firm and no longer pink, rearranging once or twice during cooking time. Let meat cups stand, covered, for 5 minutes before serving.

Cheesy Burger Meatloaf

Meatloaf:
- 1½ lbs. ground beef, crumbled
- 1 cup crushed saltine crackers
- ½ cup milk
- ¼ cup shredded Cheddar cheese
- 1 large egg
- 2 tablespoons catsup
- 2 tablespoons sour cream
- ½ teaspoon onion powder
- ½ teaspoon Worcestershire sauce
- ¼ teaspoon celery salt
- ¼ teaspoon seasoned salt

Topping:
- ¼ cup catsup
- ½ teaspoon dried parsley flakes

4 to 6 servings

Combine all the meatloaf ingredients in a medium bowl. Shape the mixture into a loaf and place in an 8 × 4-inch loaf dish. Combine the topping ingredients in a small bowl. Spread the mixture over the top of the meatloaf. Microwave at High for 13 to 18 minutes, or until meatloaf is firm and temperature in center is 145°F, rotating dish once during cooking time. Let meatloaf stand, covered, for 5 minutes before serving.

Total Cooking Time: 13 to 18 minutes

Spinach-stuffed Meatloaf ▲

Meat Mixture:
- 1 lb. ground beef, crumbled
- 1 small onion, chopped
- 1 large egg
- ½ teaspoon salt
- ¼ teaspoon pepper

Filling:
- 2 pkgs. (10 oz. each) frozen chopped spinach
- ½ teaspoon ground nutmeg
- ½ cup shredded mozzarella cheese

4 to 6 servings

1 Combine all the meat mixture ingredients in a medium bowl. Press half of the meat mixture into the bottom of an 8 × 4-inch loaf dish. Make a slight indentation lengthwise down the center of the meat layer; set aside.

2 Unwrap the spinach and place on a plate. Microwave at High for 5 to 8 minutes, or until spinach is defrosted, turning over and breaking apart once during cooking time. Drain, pressing to remove excess moisture.

3 Combine the spinach and the nutmeg in a small bowl. Sprinkle half of the spinach mixture down the center of the meat layer, then sprinkle with the cheese. Top with the remaining spinach, pressing lightly.

4 Top with the remaining meat mixture, pressing to enclose filling and seal edges. Microwave at High for 13 to 18 minutes, or until the meatloaf is firm and temperature in center is 145°F, rotating dish once during cooking time. Let meatloaf stand, covered, for 5 minutes before serving.

Total Cooking Time: 18 to 26 minutes

Artichoke Cheese Roll ➤

Meat Mixture:

1½ lbs. ground beef, crumbled
2 large eggs
⅓ cup sour cream
¼ cup seasoned dry bread crumbs
2 tablespoons sliced green onion
½ teaspoon dried basil leaves
½ teaspoon salt
¼ teaspoon pepper

Filling:

1 can (14 oz.) artichoke hearts, drained and chopped
⅓ cup shredded Monterey Jack cheese
⅓ cup shredded Cheddar cheese
¼ teaspoon dried basil leaves

4 to 6 servings

1 Combine all the meat mixture ingredients in a medium bowl. On wax paper, shape mixture into a 12 × 8-inch rectangle, ½ inch thick. Set aside. Combine all filling ingredients in a small bowl. Sprinkle meat with the filling mixture, leaving a 1-inch border on all sides.

2 Roll up loaf, starting on the short side. Lift the paper until the meat begins to roll tightly, enclosing filling. Continue to lift and peel back the paper while completing the roll. Seal edges.

3 Place the meatloaf seam-side-down in an 8 × 4-inch loaf dish. Microwave at High for 10 minutes, rotating dish after half the cooking time.

4 Microwave at 50% (Medium) for 10 to 20 minutes longer, or until meatloaf is firm and temperature in center is 145°F, rotating dish once during cooking time. Let meatloaf stand, covered, for 5 minutes before serving.

Total Cooking Time: 20 to 30 minutes

Variation:

Mushroom Cheese Roll:
Follow recipe for Artichoke Cheese Roll, except: substitute 2 cans (4 oz. each) sliced mushrooms, drained, for the artichokes.

Sauerbraten Meatloaf

1½ lbs. ground beef, crumbled
½ cup finely crushed gingersnap cookies
1 large egg
2 tablespoons red wine vinegar
2 tablespoons unseasoned dry bread crumbs
1 tablespoon packed brown sugar
½ teaspoon salt
¼ teaspoon pepper
⅛ teaspoon ground cloves

4 to 6 servings

Combine all the ingredients in a medium bowl. Shape the mixture into a loaf and place in an 8 × 4-inch loaf dish. Microwave at High for 13 to 18 minutes, or until the meatloaf is firm and temperature in center is 145°F, rotating dish once during cooking time. Let meatloaf stand, covered, for 5 minutes before serving.

Total Cooking Time: 13 to 18 minutes

Make-ahead Meatloaf Swirls

¼ cup sesame seed

Meat Mixture:
2 lbs. ground beef, crumbled
2 large eggs
½ cup seasoned dry bread crumbs
¾ teaspoon salt

Filling:
1 cup shredded mozzarella cheese
½ cup seasoned dry bread crumbs
1 can (4 oz.) sliced mushrooms, drained
¼ cup sliced green onions
¼ cup grated Parmesan cheese
1 tablespoon dried parsley flakes
1 teaspoon Italian seasoning

4 or 8 servings

Follow photo directions, below.

Total Cooking Time: 18 to 22 minutes

How to Microwave Make-ahead Meatloaf Swirls

1 Toast the sesame seed conventionally in a small skillet over medium heat. Set aside to cool. Combine all the meat mixture ingredients in a medium bowl. Set aside. Combine all the filling ingredients in a small bowl.

2 On wax paper, shape the meat mixture into a 15 × 9-inch rectangle. Sprinkle meat with the filling mixture, leaving a 1-inch border on all sides. Roll up the loaf, starting on the short side. Lift the paper until the meat begins to roll tightly, enclosing the filling. Continue to lift and peel back the paper while completing the roll.

3 Roll the meatloaf in the toasted sesame seed, pressing to coat. Slice the loaf into 8 equal pieces. Place pieces on a wax-paper-lined baking sheet and freeze until firm. Remove 4 meatloaf slices from the baking sheet and wrap in freezer paper or foil; repeat with remaining slices. Freeze for future use.

4 To serve meatloaf, unwrap one package and arrange swirls on a roasting rack. Cover with wax paper; microwave at 70% (Medium High) for 18 to 22 minutes, or until the meat is firm and no longer pink, rotating rack once or twice during cooking time. Let meatloaf swirls stand for 3 minutes before serving.

Reuben Meatloaf

Meat Mixture:

1 lb. ground beef, crumbled
1 cup soft rye bread crumbs
½ cup prepared Thousand Island dressing
1 large egg
½ teaspoon caraway seed
¼ teaspoon salt
⅛ teaspoon pepper

Filling:

1 can (8 oz.) sauerkraut
1 oz. fully cooked corned beef, chopped
½ cup shredded Swiss cheese

4 to 6 servings

Follow photo directions, right.

Total Cooking Time: 13 to 18 minutes

How to Microwave Reuben Meatloaf

1 Combine all the meat mixture ingredients in a medium bowl. Press half of the mixture into the bottom of an 8 × 4-inch loaf dish. Make a slight indentation lengthwise down the center of the meat layer.

2 Rinse and drain the sauerkraut, pressing to remove excess moisture. Combine all filling ingredients in a small bowl. Sprinkle the mixture lengthwise down the center of the meat layer. Top with the remaining meat mixture, pressing to enclose the filling and seal the edges.

3 Microwave at High for 13 to 18 minutes, or until the meatloaf is firm and temperature in center is 145°F, rotating dish once during cooking time. Let meatloaf stand, covered, for 5 minutes before serving.

Italian Meatloaf ▲

Meatloaf:
- 1 lb. ground beef, crumbled
- ½ lb. bulk Italian sausage, crumbled
- ½ cup seasoned dry bread crumbs
- ½ cup milk
- 1 large egg
- 1 teaspoon Italian seasoning
- ½ teaspoon salt
- ¼ teaspoon pepper
- ¼ teaspoon onion powder

Topping:
- 2 slices (¾ oz. each) mozzarella cheese, cut in half
- ½ teaspoon dried parsley flakes

4 to 6 servings

Combine all meatloaf ingredients in a medium bowl. Shape the mixture into a loaf and place in an 8 × 4-inch loaf dish. Microwave at High for 15 to 20 minutes, or until the meatloaf is firm and temperature in center is 165°F, rotating dish once during cooking time. Arrange cheese slices over meatloaf; sprinkle with parsley. Let meatloaf stand, covered, for 5 minutes before serving. (Cheese will melt during standing time.)

Total Cooking Time: 15 to 20 minutes

Scandinavian Meatloaf

- 1½ lbs. ground beef, crumbled
- ¾ cup milk
- ⅔ cup instant mashed potato flakes
- 1 large egg
- ½ teaspoon onion powder
- ½ teaspoon salt
- ½ teaspoon dried dill weed
- ½ teaspoon dried summer savory leaves
- ⅛ teaspoon ground nutmeg

4 to 6 servings

Combine all the ingredients in a medium bowl. Shape the mixture into a loaf and place in an 8 × 4-inch loaf dish. Microwave at High for 13 to 18 minutes, or until the meatloaf is firm and temperature in center is 145°F, rotating dish once during cooking time. Let meatloaf stand, covered, for 5 minutes before serving.

Total Cooking Time: 13 to 18 minutes

Family Favorite Meatloaf

1½ lbs. ground beef, crumbled
1 can (6 oz.) tomato juice
½ cup uncooked quick-cooking rolled oats
1 large egg
¼ cup chopped onion
1 teaspoon dried marjoram leaves
½ teaspoon salt
½ teaspoon ground sage
⅛ teaspoon pepper

4 to 6 servings

Combine all the ingredients in a medium bowl. Shape the mixture into a loaf and place in an 8 × 4-inch loaf dish. Microwave at High for 13 to 18 minutes, or until the meatloaf is firm and temperature in center is 145°F, rotating dish once during cooking time. Let meatloaf stand, covered, for 5 minutes before serving.

Total Cooking Time: 13 to 18 minutes

Sunday Best Meatloaf ▲

1½ lbs. ground beef, crumbled
1 cup soft bread crumbs
½ cup milk
½ cup instant mashed potato flakes
⅓ cup finely chopped onion
¼ cup finely chopped celery
¼ cup finely chopped green pepper
1 large egg
1 jar (2 oz.) chopped pimientos, drained
1 tablespoon Worcestershire sauce
1 teaspoon dry mustard
½ teaspoon salt
¼ teaspoon pepper

4 to 6 servings

Combine all the ingredients in a medium bowl. Shape the mixture into a loaf and place in an 8 × 4-inch loaf dish. Microwave at High for 13 to 18 minutes, or until the meatloaf is firm and temperature in center is 145°F, rotating dish once during cooking time. Let meatloaf stand, covered, for 5 minutes before serving.

Total Cooking Time: 13 to 18 minutes

Smokey Barbecue Loaf

- 1 lb. ground beef, crumbled
- ¼ lb. bulk pork sausage, crumbled
- ½ cup unseasoned dry bread crumbs
- 1 large egg
- ¼ cup milk
- 2 tablespoons chili sauce
- 1 tablespoon instant minced onion
- ¾ teaspoon salt
- ¼ teaspoon liquid smoke flavoring
- ⅛ teaspoon cayenne
- 3 tablespoons prepared barbecue sauce (optional)

4 to 6 servings

1 Combine all the ingredients, except barbecue sauce, in a medium bowl. Shape the mixture into a loaf and place in an 8×4-inch loaf dish. Spread barbecue sauce evenly over the top of the meatloaf.

2 Microwave at High for 15 to 20 minutes, or until the meatloaf is firm and temperature in center is 165°F, rotating dish once during cooking time. Let meatloaf stand, covered, for 5 minutes before serving.

Total Cooking Time: 15 to 20 minutes

Curried Meatloaf

Meatloaf:

1½ lbs. ground beef, crumbled
1 can (8 oz.) crushed pineapple
½ cup unseasoned dry bread crumbs
2 large eggs
¼ cup chopped green pepper
¼ cup chopped onion
1½ teaspoons curry powder
1 teaspoon Worcestershire sauce
½ teaspoon salt
⅛ teaspoon cayenne

Topping:

⅓ cup mayonnaise or salad dressing
1 teaspoon prepared mustard
¼ teaspoon curry powder

4 to 6 servings

1 Combine all the meatloaf ingredients in a medium bowl. Shape the mixture into a loaf and place in an 8 × 4-inch loaf dish. Microwave at High for 13 to 18 minutes, or until the meatloaf is firm and temperature in center is 145°F, rotating dish once during cooking time.

2 Let meatloaf stand, covered, for 5 minutes. Blend all topping ingredients in a small bowl. Serve topping with meatloaf slices. If desired, garnish servings with sliced green onions.

Total Cooking Time: 13 to 18 minutes

Casseroles & One-dish Meals

Casseroles & One-dish Meals

*All-in-one timesavers
your whole family will love*

Cheesy Mac & Burger Casserole

⅓ cup chopped onion
¼ cup chopped green pepper
½ lb. ground beef, crumbled
1 pkg. (7 oz.) uncooked elbow macaroni,
   prepared as directed on pkg.
1 can (16 oz.) whole tomatoes, drained
   and cut up
1 pkg. (8 oz.) pasteurized process cheese
   spread loaf, cut into ¾-inch cubes
¼ cup milk
½ teaspoon salt
¼ teaspoon dried marjoram leaves
⅛ teaspoon pepper

4 to 6 servings

1 Combine the onion and green pepper in a
2-quart casserole. Cover; microwave at High
for 2 to 3 minutes, or until vegetables are tender.
Add the ground beef; stir to combine. Re-cover.

2 Microwave at High for 2 to 4 minutes, or until
the meat is no longer pink, stirring to break
apart once during cooking time. Drain. Stir in
macaroni and remaining ingredients. Re-cover.

3 Microwave at High for 6 to 8 minutes, or until
the mixture is hot and the cheese is melted,
stirring twice during cooking time. If desired,
sprinkle casserole with paprika before serving.

Total Cooking Time: 10 to 15 minutes

Shepherds' Pie (pictured on pages 78-79)

1 lb. ground beef, crumbled
1 medium onion, chopped
1 can (10¾ oz.) condensed tomato soup
1 teaspoon Worcestershire sauce
½ teaspoon salt
¼ teaspoon dried basil leaves
⅛ teaspoon pepper

1 pkg. (10 oz.) frozen peas and carrots
3 cups hot cooked mashed potatoes
1 cup shredded Cheddar cheese

4 to 6 servings

Follow photo directions, below.

Total Cooking Time: 14 to 19 minutes

How to Microwave Shepherds' Pie

1 Place the ground beef and onion in a 2-quart casserole. Microwave at High for 4 to 7 minutes, or until meat is no longer pink, stirring to break apart once or twice during cooking time. Drain.

2 Stir in the tomato soup, Worcestershire sauce, salt, basil and pepper. Press mixture into an even layer in the casserole. Set aside.

3 Place the frozen vegetables in a small bowl. Microwave at High for 4 to 5 minutes, or until vegetables are defrosted, stirring to break apart once during cooking time.

4 Sprinkle the peas and carrots in an even layer over ground beef mixture. Spoon mounds of potatoes over vegetables; sprinkle with cheese. Microwave at High for 6 to 7 minutes, or until the cheese is melted and casserole is hot, rotating casserole once during cooking time.

Crunchy Taco Bake ▲

1 lb. ground beef, crumbled
2 tablespoons dried onion flakes
1 can (16 oz.) tomato sauce
1 can (15 oz.) hot chili with beans
1 can (6 oz.) tomato paste
1½ teaspoons chili powder
½ teaspoon salt
2 cups coarsely crushed corn chips
1 cup shredded Cheddar cheese

4 to 6 servings

1 In a 2-quart casserole, microwave the ground beef and onion at High for 4 to 7 minutes, or until meat is no longer pink, stirring to break apart once or twice during cooking time. Drain.

2 Stir in the tomato sauce, chili, tomato paste, chili powder and salt. Microwave at High for 6 to 10 minutes, or until the mixture is hot and flavors are blended, stirring once or twice during cooking time.

3 Top casserole with the corn chips and sprinkle with cheese. Microwave at High for 1½ to 3½ minutes, or until the cheese melts.

Total Cooking Time: 11½ to 20½ minutes

Mexican Beef & Macaroni

1 lb. ground beef, crumbled
½ cup chopped onion
½ cup chopped green pepper
1 can (16 oz.) tomato sauce
1 cup uncooked elbow macaroni, prepared as directed on pkg.
2 teaspoons chili powder
¾ teaspoon salt
½ to 1 teaspoon ground cumin
⅛ teaspoon pepper

Topping:
1 cup crushed corn chips
½ cup finely shredded Cheddar cheese

4 to 6 servings

1 Place the ground beef, onion and green pepper in a 1½-quart casserole. Cover; microwave at High for 5 to 8 minutes, or until the meat is no longer pink, stirring to break apart once or twice during cooking time. Drain.

2 Stir in the remaining ingredients, except topping. Re-cover. Microwave at High for 8 to 10 minutes, or until the flavors are blended, stirring once during cooking time.

3 Sprinkle casserole with corn chips and cheese. Microwave at High for 30 seconds to 1 minute, or until the cheese melts.

Total Cooking Time: 13½ to 19 minutes

Beef Enchiladas ▲

½ lb. ground beef, crumbled
1½ teaspoons instant minced onion
½ teaspoon salt
2 cups shredded Cheddar cheese, divided
1 can (10 oz.) mild enchilada sauce, divided
1 tablespoon chopped canned or fresh green chilies (optional)
6 corn tortillas (7-inch diameter) softened as directed on pkg.

4 to 6 servings

1 Place the ground beef, onion and salt in a 1-quart casserole. Microwave at High for 2 to 4 minutes, or until the meat is no longer pink, stirring to break apart once or twice during cooking time. Drain.

2 Stir in half the cheese, ¼ cup of the enchilada sauce and the chilies. Spoon a scant ⅓ cup of the meat mixture down the center of each tortilla; roll up to enclose filling. Place enchiladas seam-side-down in a 9-inch square baking dish.

3 Pour the remaining enchilada sauce over the filled tortillas and top with remaining cheese. Microwave at High for 6½ to 7½ minutes, or until the cheese is melted and enchiladas are hot, rotating dish once or twice during cooking time. If desired, top with shredded lettuce and sour cream before serving.

Total Cooking Time: 8½ to 11½ minutes

Chili Rice

1 lb. ground beef, crumbled
½ cup chopped onion
½ cup chopped green pepper
⅛ teaspoon instant minced garlic
1 can (16 oz.) whole tomatoes, cut up
1 can (15 oz.) kidney beans, drained
1 cup uncooked instant rice
1 to 2 teaspoons chili powder
1 teaspoon salt
½ teaspoon sugar
1 cup shredded Cheddar cheese

4 to 6 servings

1 In a 2-quart casserole, place the ground beef, onion, green pepper and garlic. Cover, and microwave at High for 4 to 8 minutes, or until the meat is no longer pink and the vegetables are tender, stirring to break apart once or twice during cooking time. Drain.

2 Add the remaining ingredients, except the cheese. Cover; microwave at High for 10 to 13 minutes, or until the rice is tender, stirring once during cooking time.

3 Sprinkle casserole with cheese; microwave at High for 2 to 3 minutes, or until cheese melts.

Total Cooking Time: 16 to 24 minutes

Manicotti

8 uncooked manicotti shells, prepared as
    directed on pkg.
1 pkg. (10 oz.) frozen chopped spinach
½ lb. ground beef, crumbled
¼ cup chopped onion
½ cup soft bread crumbs
3 tablespoons grated Parmesan cheese, divided
1 large egg
¼ teaspoon salt
⅛ teaspoon pepper
1 can (16 oz.) tomato sauce
½ teaspoon sugar
½ teaspoon Italian seasoning
½ cup ricotta cheese
1 tablespoon dried parsley flakes

4 to 6 servings

Follow photo directions, below.

Total Cooking Time: 13 to 20 minutes

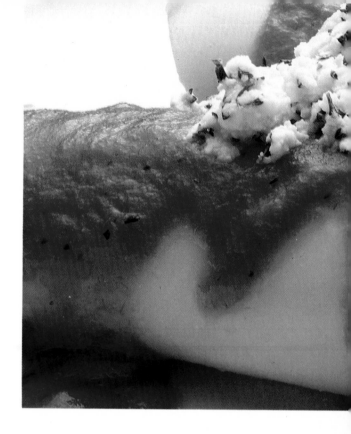

How to Microwave Manicotti

1 Place the prepared manicotti shells between
damp paper towels; set aside. Unwrap the
spinach and place on plate. Microwave spinach
at High for 4 to 6 minutes, or until defrosted,
turning over and breaking apart once during
cooking time. Drain, pressing to remove excess
moisture. Set aside.

2 Place the ground beef and onion in a 1-quart
casserole. Microwave at High for 2 to 4
minutes, or until the meat is no longer pink,
stirring to break apart once during cooking time.
Drain. Add the bread crumbs, 2 tablespoons of
the Parmesan cheese, the egg, salt and pepper.
Stir in the spinach.

3 Fill manicotti shells evenly with meat mixture. Arrange stuffed shells in a 10-inch square casserole. Set aside. In a medium bowl, mix the tomato sauce, sugar and Italian seasoning. Pour mixture over the stuffed manicotti shells.

4 In a small bowl, mix the ricotta cheese, parsley and remaining Parmesan cheese. Drop spoonfuls of the mixture randomly over sauce. Cover with plastic wrap; microwave at High for 7 to 10 minutes, or until temperature in center is 145°F, rotating dish once during cooking time.

Hamburger Bean Pot

4 slices bacon, chopped
1 lb. ground beef, crumbled
1 medium apple, peeled and finely chopped
½ cup chopped onion
1 can (16 oz.) pork and beans in tomato sauce
¼ cup molasses
¼ cup prepared barbecue sauce
1 cup broken corn chips

4 to 6 servings

1 Place the bacon in a 2-quart casserole and cover with a paper towel. Microwave at High for 4½ to 7 minutes, or until bacon is crisp and golden brown. Drain.

2 Add the ground beef, apple and onion. Cover; microwave at High for 6 to 8 minutes, or until the meat is no longer pink, stirring to break apart once or twice during cooking time. Drain.

3 Add the remaining ingredients, except the corn chips. Cover; microwave at High for 4 to 6 minutes, or until hot and bubbly, stirring once during cooking time. Sprinkle casserole with corn chips before serving.

Total Cooking Time: 14½ to 21 minutes

Four-layer Dinner ▲

1 pkg. (10 oz.) frozen chopped spinach
2 cups hot cooked rice
1 cup shredded Swiss cheese, divided
1 large egg, slightly beaten
1 lb. ground beef, crumbled
1 can (6 oz.) tomato paste
1 pkg. (.75 oz.) mushroom gravy mix
⅔ cup water
¼ teaspoon dried basil leaves

4 to 6 servings

1 Unwrap the spinach and place on a plate. Microwave at High for 4 to 6 minutes, or until spinach is defrosted, turning over and breaking apart once during cooking time. Drain, pressing to remove excess moisture. Set aside.

2 Combine the rice, ½ cup of the Swiss cheese and the egg in a medium bowl. Press the rice mixture evenly into the bottom of a 9-inch square baking dish. Microwave at High for 4 to 5 minutes, or until the mixture is set, rotating dish once during cooking time. Set aside.

3 Place the ground beef in a 2-quart casserole. Microwave at High for 4 to 7 minutes, or until the meat is no longer pink, stirring to break apart once or twice during cooking time. Drain. Add the tomato paste, gravy mix, water and basil; mix well.

4 Spoon the meat mixture evenly over the rice. Top with the spinach and remaining cheese. Microwave at High for 5 minutes. Rotate dish; microwave at 50% (Medium) for 3½ to 5 minutes longer, or until the cheese is melted and temperature in center is 145°F.

Total Cooking Time: 20½ to 28 minutes

Chinese Hamburger Hash ➤

1 medium onion, chopped
½ cup thinly sliced celery
½ cup shredded carrot
½ lb. lean ground beef, crumbled
1 can (10¾ oz.) condensed cream of
    mushroom soup
1 cup hot tap water
½ cup uncooked instant rice
2 tablespoons soy sauce
⅛ teaspoon pepper

4 to 6 servings

1 In a 1½-quart casserole, combine the onion, celery and carrot. Cover; microwave at High for 4 to 6 minutes, or until the vegetables are tender, stirring once during cooking time. Add the ground beef; re-cover.

2 Microwave at High for 2 to 4 minutes, or until the meat is no longer pink, stirring to break apart once during cooking time. Stir in remaining ingredients; re-cover.

3 Microwave at High for 8 to 10 minutes, or until rice is tender. Let stand for 3 to 5 minutes. If desired, serve hash over chow mein noodles.

Total Cooking Time: 14 to 20 minutes

Stuffed Green Peppers

4 large green peppers (8 oz. each)
1 lb. lean ground beef, crumbled
½ cup chopped onion
1 cup hot cooked rice
1 can (8 oz.) whole tomatoes, drained
    and cut up
1 can (6 oz.) tomato paste
1 teaspoon seasoned salt
⅛ teaspoon instant minced garlic
4 slices (¾ oz. each) pasteurized process
    American cheese, each cut into 4 strips

4 servings

1 Cut a thin slice from the top of each pepper; discard. Core and seed peppers, and arrange cut-sides-up in a 9-inch square baking dish.

2 In a 2-quart casserole, microwave the ground beef and onion at High for 4 to 7 minutes, or until meat is no longer pink, stirring to break apart once or twice during cooking time. Drain. Add the remaining ingredients, except the cheese, and mix well.

3 Divide meat mixture into 4 portions and place 1 portion in each green pepper. Cover with plastic wrap; microwave at High for 8 to 15 minutes, or until peppers are tender-crisp, rotating dish once during cooking time.

4 Top each pepper with 4 criss-crossed strips of cheese. Microwave at 50% (Medium) for 1 to 2 minutes, or until the cheese melts.

Total Cooking Time: 13 to 24 minutes

Vegetable Beef Pies ➤

1 pkg. (15 oz.) refrigerated rolled pie crusts
Filling:
1 cup shredded carrot
1 cup shredded potato
¼ cup chopped onion
1 tablespoon butter or margarine
2 teaspoons dried parsley flakes
¼ teaspoon caraway seed
¼ teaspoon salt
⅛ teaspoon pepper
½ lb. ground beef, crumbled

4 servings

Heat conventional oven to 375°F. Remove the pie crusts from package and let stand at room temperature for 15 minutes. Place all the filling ingredients, except the ground beef, in a 1½-quart casserole. Cover; microwave at High for 4½ to 5½ minutes, or until the vegetables are tender, stirring once or twice during cooking time. Continue with photo directions, below.

Total Cooking Time: 31½ to 39½ minutes

How to Microwave Vegetable Beef Pies

1 Add the ground beef to casserole. Microwave at High for 2 to 4 minutes, or until the meat is no longer pink, stirring to break apart once or twice during cooking time. Set aside.

2 Unfold the rolled crusts. Cut crusts in half to yield 4 half-moon pieces. Spoon a heaping ½ cup of the meat mixture toward one end of each half-circle.

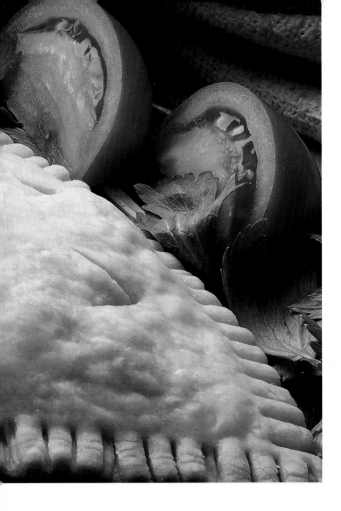

Hamburger Potato Casserole

1 lb. ground beef, crumbled
4 cups thinly sliced potatoes
1 can (10¾ oz.) condensed vegetable
  beef soup
½ teaspoon salt
1 can (3 oz.) French-fried onions

4 servings

1 In a 2-quart casserole, microwave the ground beef at High for 4 to 7 minutes, or until meat is no longer pink, stirring to break apart once or twice during cooking time. Drain.

2 Stir in the potatoes, soup and salt. Cover, and microwave at High for 15 to 20 minutes, or until the potatoes are fork-tender, stirring 2 or 3 times during cooking.

3 Sprinkle the French-fried onions over the casserole. Microwave at High for 1½ to 3 minutes, or until the casserole is hot.

Total Cooking Time: 20½ to 30 minutes

3 Fold over opposite end of crust to enclose filling; press edges together with a fork to seal. Arrange the pies on a baking sheet.

4 Make several small slits in the top of each pie. Bake meat pies for 25 to 30 minutes, or until golden brown.

American Lasagne

12 uncooked lasagne noodles, prepared as
    directed on pkg.

Sauce:

½ lb. ground beef, crumbled

⅛ teaspoon garlic powder

1 can (16 oz.) whole tomatoes, drained
    and chopped

1 can (6 oz.) tomato paste

¾ teaspoon Italian seasoning

½ teaspoon salt

½ teaspoon dried oregano leaves

¼ teaspoon pepper

Filling:

2 cups small curd cottage cheese

2 large eggs

¾ cup grated Parmesan cheese, divided

2 cups shredded mozzarella cheese

1 tablespoon snipped fresh parsley (optional)

                    6 to 8 servings

Follow photo directions, below.

Total Cooking Time: 22 to 28 minutes

How to Microwave American Lasagne

1 Rinse lasagne noodles and let stand in warm
water while preparing sauce. Place ground
beef in a 1-quart casserole. Add garlic powder.
Cover; microwave at High for 2 to 4 minutes, or
until meat is no longer pink, stirring to break
apart once during cooking time. Drain.

2 Stir in remaining sauce ingredients. Re-cover.
Microwave at High for 5 minutes, stirring once
during cooking time. Set aside. Combine cottage
cheese, eggs and ¼ cup of the Parmesan cheese
in a food processor or blender. Process until
smooth; set aside.

3 Drain lasagne noodles on paper towels. In a 10-inch square casserole, layer 4 noodles, half of the mozzarella cheese, half of the cottage cheese mixture and half of the sauce. Repeat once. Top with the remaining 4 noodles; sprinkle with remaining Parmesan cheese. Cover with plastic wrap.

4 Microwave at High for 5 minutes. Rotate casserole; microwave at 70% (Medium High) for 10 to 14 minutes longer, or until temperature in center is 145°F, rotating casserole twice during cooking time. Let lasagne stand for 10 minutes; sprinkle with parsley before serving.

Layered Spinach Bake

1 pkg. (10 oz.) frozen chopped spinach
1 lb. ground beef, crumbled
1 tablespoon instant minced onion
⅛ teaspoon garlic powder
1 jar (15½ oz.) spaghetti sauce
¼ cup unseasoned dry bread crumbs, divided
1 cup cottage cheese
1 large egg
⅛ teaspoon pepper
1 cup shredded mozzarella cheese
2 tablespoons grated Parmesan cheese

4 to 6 servings

Follow photo directions, right.

Total Cooking Time: 21 to 32 minutes

Taste Tip:
*For variety or convenience, prepare Layered
Spinach Bake using Cheddar cheese in place
of the mozzarella.*

How to Microwave
Layered Spinach Bake

1 Unwrap the spinach and place on a plate.
Microwave at High for 4 to 6 minutes, or until
defrosted, turning over and breaking apart once
during cooking time. Drain, pressing to remove
excess moisture. Set aside.

2 Place the ground beef, onion and garlic powder in a 2-quart casserole. Microwave at High for 4 to 7 minutes, or until the meat is no longer pink, stirring to break apart once or twice during cooking time. Drain.

3 Stir in the spaghetti sauce. Cover; microwave at High for 2 to 4 minutes, or until mixture is hot and bubbly, stirring once during cooking time. Stir in 2 tablespoons of the bread crumbs. Set aside.

4 In a medium bowl, combine the spinach, remaining 2 tablespoons of bread crumbs, cottage cheese, egg and pepper. Spread half the meat mixture in the bottom of a 9-inch square baking dish. Top with the spinach mixture, and sprinkle with mozzarella cheese. Top with the remaining meat mixture.

5 Sprinkle with Parmesan cheese. Microwave at High for 3 minutes. Microwave at 50% (Medium) for 8 to 12 minutes longer, or until temperature in center is 145°F, rotating dish once or twice during cooking time. Let stand for 5 minutes before serving.

INDEX

A

American Lasagne, 90
Artichoke Cheese Roll, with
  Variation, 69

B

Bacon,
  Bacon Cheese Burgers, 12
  Bacon-wrapped Mini Meatloaves, 64
  Wild Rice & Bacon Burgers, 19
Barbecued,
  Smokey Barbecue Loaf, 76
  Southern Barbecue Burgers, 19
Basic Hamburgers, 11
Basic Salisbury Steak, 13
Basic Stuffed Burgers, 15
Beans,
  Beef & Bean Burritos, 21
  Hamburger & Bean Soup, 29
  Hamburger Bean Pot, 86
Beef,
  Beef & Bean Burritos, 21
  Beef Enchiladas, 83
  Creamy Beef & Sausage Soup, with
    Variation, 30
  Creamy Beef, Sausage & Potato
    Soup, 30
  Mexican Beef & Macaroni, 82
  Vegetable Beef Pies, 88
Beefy Mushroom Potato Topper, 42
Beefy Spaghetti Soup, 28
Browning,
  How to Brown Ground Beef Patties, 6
Burgers,
  Bacon Cheese Burgers, 12
  Basic Hamburgers, 11
  Basic Stuffed Burgers, 15
  Chili Burgers, 19
  Open-face Pizza Burgers, 18
  Southern Barbecue Burgers, 19
  Stuffed Burgers Mexican Style, 17
  Stuffed Italian Burgers, 16
  Stuffed Mushroom Burgers, 17
  Stuffed Pizza Burgers, 16
  Vegie Burgers, 12
  Wild Rice & Bacon Burgers, 19
Burritos,
  Beef & Bean Burritos, 21

C

Cajun Hamburger Stew, 35
Carrots,
  Meatballs with Potatoes & Carrots, 55
Casseroles & One-dish Meals, 78-93
  American Lasagne, 90
  Beef Enchiladas, 83

Cheesy Mac & Burger Casserole, 80
Chili Rice, 83
Chinese Hamburger Hash, 87
Crunchy Taco Bake, 82
Four-layer Dinner, 86
Hamburger Bean Pot, 86
Hamburger Potato Casserole, 89
Layered Spinach Bake, 92
Manicotti, 84
Mexican Beef & Macaroni, 82
Shepherds' Pie, 81
Stuffed Green Peppers, 87
Vegetable Beef Pies, 88
Cheese,
  Artichoke Cheese Roll, with
    Variation, 69
  Bacon Cheese Burgers, 12
  Mushroom & Cheese Stuffed Meat
    Cups, 66
  Mushroom Cheese Roll, 69
  Cheesy Burger Meatloaf, 68
  Cheesy Mac & Burger Casserole, 80
Chili, 33
  Chili Burgers, 19
  Chili Rice, 83
  Italian Chili, 33
Chinese Hamburger Hash, 87
Coney Island Sauce, 44
Creamy Beef & Sausage Soup, with
  Variation, 30
Creamy Beef, Sausage & Potato
  Soup, 30
Creamy Dill Meatballs, with
  Variation, 58
Creamy Herb Meatballs, 58
Crunchy Taco Bake, 82
Curried Meatloaf, 77

D

Defrosting,
  How to Defrost Ground Beef, 6
  How to Defrost Ground Beef Patties, 6
Dill,
  Creamy Dill Meatballs, with
    Variation, 58

E

Enchiladas,
  Beef Enchiladas, 83

F

Family Favorite Meatloaf, 75
Four-layer Dinner, 86

CY DE COSSE INCORPORATED
Chairman: Cy DeCosse
President: James B. Maus
Executive Vice President: William B. Jones

CREDITS
Design, Production & Photography:
  Cy DeCosse Incorporated
Art Directors: Barb Falk, Bill Nelson
Project Manager: Lynette Reber
Home Economists: Peggy Lamb, Jill Crum,
  Kathy Weber
Production Manager: Jim Bindas
Assistant Production Manager: Julie Churchill
Copy Editor: Bryan Trandem
Typesetting: Jennie Smith, Linda Schloegel
Production Staff: Michelle Joy, Yelena
  Konrardy, Lisa Rosenthal, David
  Schelitzche, Cathleen Shannon,
  Nik Wogstad
Photographers: Rex Irmen, Tony Kubat,
  John Lauenstein, Mette Nielsen
Food Stylists: Teresa Ernst, Susan Sinon,
  Lynn Bachman, Lynn Boldt, Suzanne
  Finley, Carol Grones, Robin Krause
Special Microwave Consultant:
  Barbara Methven
Color Separations: Spectrum, Inc.
Printing: R.R. Donnelley & Sons (287)

G

Green Peppers,
Meatballs with Tomato & Green
Pepper Sauce, 50
Stuffed Green Peppers, 87
Stuffed Pepper Stew, 37
Ground Beef,
How to Brown Ground Beef Patties, 6
How to Defrost Ground Beef, 6
How to Defrost Ground Beef Patties, 6
How to Microwave Grease-free
Ground Beef, 7
Storing, 5

H

Hamburger & Bean Soup, 29
Hamburger Bean Pot, 86
Hamburger Potato Casserole, 89
Hamburger Stroganoff, 44
Hamburger-Vegetable Soup, 27
Hamburgers,
Bacon Cheese Burgers, 12
Basic Hamburgers, 11
Basic Stuffed Burgers, 15
Chili Burgers, 19
Open-face Pizza Burgers, 18
Southern Barbecue Burgers, 19
Stuffed Burgers Mexican Style, 17
Stuffed Italian Burgers, 16
Stuffed Mushroom Burgers, 17
Stuffed Pizza Burgers, 16
Vegie Burgers, 12
Wild Rice & Bacon Burgers, 19
Hash,
Chinese Hamburger Hash, 87
Hearty Winter Soup, 27
Herbs,
Creamy Herb Meatballs, 58
Herb Meatloaf, 66
Meatballs with Creamy Herb
Sauce, 54
Hoagies,
Italian Meatball Sandwich, 20
Meatball Hoagie, with Variation, 20

I

Italian Chili, 33
Italian Hamburger & Vegetable
Soup, 29
Italian Meat Sauce, 45
Italian Meatball Sandwich, 20
Italian Meatloaf, 74

K

Kabobs,
Mediterranean Meatball Kabobs, 56

L

Lasagne,
American Lasagne, 90
Layered Spinach Bake, 92

M

Macaroni,
Cheesy Mac & Burger Casserole, 80
Mexican Beef & Macaroni, 82
Make-ahead Meatloaf Swirls, 70
Manicotti, 84
Meatballs, 46-59
Creamy Dill Meatballs, with
Variation, 58
Creamy Herb Meatballs, 58
Italian Meatball Sandwich, 20
Meatball Hoagie, with Variation, 20
Meatball Stew, 33
Meatballs & Tomato Sauce, 48
Meatballs with Creamy Herb
Sauce, 54
Meatballs with Potatoes & Carrots, 55
Meatballs with Savory Rice, 54
Meatballs with Tomato & Green
Pepper Sauce, 50
Mediterranean Meatball Kabobs, 56
Middle Eastern Meatballs, 52
Rigatoni & Meatballs, 49
Snappy Glazed Meatballs, 52
Swedish Meatballs, 51
Sweet & Sour Meatballs, 59
Traditional Meatballs, 48
Meatloaf, 60-77
Artichoke Cheese Roll, with
Variation, 69
Bacon-wrapped Mini Meatloaves, 64
Cheesy Burger Meatloaf, 68
Curried Meatloaf, 77
Family Favorite Meatloaf, 75
Herb Meatloaf, 66
Italian Meatloaf, 74
Make-ahead Meatloaf Swirls, 70
Mushroom & Cheese Stuffed Meat
Cups, 66
Mushroom Cheese Roll, 69
Reuben Meatloaf, 73
Sauerbraten Meatloaf, 69
Scandinavian Meatloaf, 74
Smokey Barbecue Loaf, 76
Spinach-stuffed Meatloaf, 68
Stuffed Meat Cups, with Filling
Variation, 66
Sunday Best Meatloaf, 75
Traditional Meatloaf, 62
Wild Rice Stuffed Meatloaf, 65
Mediterranean Meatball Kabobs, 56
Mexican Beef & Macaroni, 82

Mexican Pizza, 21
Middle Eastern Meatballs, 52
Mushrooms,
Beefy Mushroom Potato Topper, 42
Mushroom & Cheese Stuffed Meat
Cups, 66
Mushroom Cheese Roll, 69
Stuffed Mushroom Burgers, 17

O

One-dish Meals,
see: Casseroles & One-dish
Meals, 78-93
Open-face Pizza Burgers, 18
Open-face Salisbury Steak, 13

P

Patties,
How to Brown Ground Beef Patties, 6
How to Defrost Ground Beef Patties, 6
Peppers,
Meatballs with Tomato & Green
Pepper Sauce, 50
Stuffed Green Peppers, 87
Stuffed Pepper Stew, 37
Picadillo, 43
Pies,
Shepherds' Pie, 81
Vegetable Beef Pies, 88
Pizza,
Mexican Pizza, 21
Open-face Pizza Burgers, 18
Pizza Potato Topper, 41
Stuffed Pizza Burgers, 16
Potatoes,
Beefy Mushroom Potato Topper, 42
Creamy Beef, Sausage & Potato
Soup, 30
Hamburger Potato Casserole, 89
Meatballs with Potatoes & Carrots, 55
Pizza Potato Topper, 41
Taco Potatoes, 43

Q

Quick Hamburger & Vegetable
Soup, 29

R

Reuben Meatloaf, 73
Rice,
Chili Rice, 83
Meatballs with Savory Rice, 54

Tomato, Hamburger & Rice Soup, 28
Wild Rice & Bacon Burgers, 19
Wild Rice Stuffed Meatloaf, 65
Rigatoni & Meatballs, 49

S

Salisbury Steaks,
  Basic Salisbury Steak, 13
  Open-face Salisbury Steak, 13
Sandwiches & Snacks, 8-23
  Bacon Cheese Burgers, 12
  Basic Hamburgers, 11
  Basic Salisbury Steak, 13
  Basic Stuffed Burgers, 15
  Beef & Bean Burritos, 21
  Chili Burgers, 19
  Italian Meatball Sandwich, 20
  Meatball Hoagie, with Variation, 20
  Mexican Pizza, 21
  Open-face Pizza Burgers, 18
  Open-face Salisbury Steak, 13
  Southern Barbecue Burgers, 19
  Stuffed Burgers Mexican Style, 17
  Stuffed Italian Burgers, 16
  Stuffed Mushroom Burgers, 17
  Stuffed Pizza Burgers, 16
  Tostadas, 23
  Vegie Burgers, 12
  Wild Rice & Bacon Burgers, 19
Sauces & Toppings, 38-45
  Coney Island Sauce, 44
  Hamburger Stroganoff, 44
  Italian Meat Sauce, 45
  Meatballs & Tomato Sauce, 48
  Meatballs with Creamy Herb
    Sauce, 54
  Meatballs with Tomato & Green
    Pepper Sauce, 50
Sauerbraten Meatloaf, 69
Sausage,
  Creamy Beef & Sausage Soup, with
    Variation, 30
  Creamy Beef, Sausage & Potato
    Soup, 30
Scandinavian Meatloaf, 74
Shepherds' Pie, 81
Smokey Barbecue Loaf, 76
Snacks,
  see: Sandwiches & Snacks, 8-23
Snappy Glazed Meatballs, 52
Soups & Stews, 24-37
  Beefy Spaghetti Soup, 28
  Creamy Beef & Sausage Soup, with
    Variation, 30
  Creamy Beef, Sausage & Potato
    Soup, 30
  Hamburger & Bean Soup, 29
  Hamburger-Vegetable Soup, 27

Hearty Winter Soup, 27
  Italian Hamburger & Vegetable
    Soup, 29
  Quick Hamburger & Vegetable
    Soup, 29
  Tomato, Hamburger & Rice Soup, 28
Southern Barbecue Burgers, 19
Spaghetti,
  Beefy Spaghetti Soup, 28
Spinach,
  Layered Spinach Bake, 92
  Spinach-stuffed Meatloaf, 68
Steaks,
  Basic Salisbury Steak, 13
  Open-face Salisbury Steak, 13
Stews,
  Cajun Hamburger Stew, 35
  Chili, 33
  Italian Chili, 33
  Meatball Stew, 33
  Soups & Stews, 24-37
  Stuffed Pepper Stew, 37
  Zucchini Stew, 35
Storing Ground Beef, 5
Stroganoff,
  Hamburger Stroganoff, 44
Stuffed Burgers,
  Basic Stuffed Burgers, 15
  Stuffed Burgers Mexican Style, 17
  Stuffed Italian Burgers, 16
  Stuffed Mushroom Burgers, 17
  Stuffed Pizza Burgers, 16
Stuffed Green Peppers, 87
Stuffed Meat Cups, with Filling
  Variation, 66
Stuffed Pepper Stew, 37
Sunday Best Meatloaf, 75
Swedish Meatballs, 51
Sweet & Sour Meatballs, 59

T

Tacos,
  Crunchy Taco Bake, 82
  Taco Potatoes, 43
Tomatoes,
  Meatballs & Tomato Sauce, 48
  Meatballs with Tomato & Green
    Pepper Sauce, 50
  Tomato, Hamburger & Rice Soup, 28
Toppings,
  Beefy Mushroom Potato Topper, 42
  Picadillo, 43
  Pizza Potato Topper, 41
  Sauces & Toppings, 38-45
  Taco Potatoes, 43
Tostadas, 23
Traditional Meatballs, 48
Traditional Meatloaf, 62

V

Vegetables,
  Hamburger-Vegetable Soup, 27
  Italian Hamburger & Vegetable
    Soup, 29
  Quick Hamburger & Vegetable
    Soup, 29
  Vegetable Beef Pies, 88
  Vegie Burgers, 12

W

Wild Rice & Bacon Burgers, 19
Wild Rice Stuffed Meatloaf, 65

Z

Zucchini Stew, 35